# NAT'I & INT'L GODDESS FESTIVAL 2025

# AN ANTHOLOGY
# CELEBRATING WOMEN
# DURING
# WOMENS HISTORY MONTH

National Beat Poetry Foundation, Inc

Published by
New Generation Beat Publications

Copyright 2025

by
New Generation Beat Publications

All Rights Reserved

ISBN: 978-1-957654-14-0

Debbie Tosun Kilday - Editing & Cover Design.

Human Error Publishing - Editing & Formatting

All poems submitted by the authors in this book are owned and copyrighted by each individual author and remain theirs.

NBPF thanks each author for including their work here.

New Generation Beat Publications asks that no part of this publication be reproduced or transmitted in any form or by any means electronic or mechanical, including photocopy, recording or information storage or retrieval system without permission in writing from New Generation Beat Publications. The reasons for this are to help support publisher and the artists

## TABLE OF CONTENTS

Trier Ward - Isis is Unconquerable     10

Ron Whitehead - Redemption     11
for Jinn Bug

Christen Lee - This Is Only the Beginning     14

Mikayla Cyr - Skin Deep     16

Binod Dawadi - Woman     17

Tajalla Qureshi - Woman: The Goddess of Poetry     18

Megha Sood - Homage to My Hair     19
After Lucille Clifton

Belinda Subraman - Christmas in "Independent Living"     21

Chivas Sandage - Persephone's Tattoo     23

B. Elizabeth Beck - Woman Rising     24

Dinara Orazbekova - Paradise under the feet of our     25
mothers.

Catherine Lee - A Rap Upon The Queen's Attraction     26

Puma Perl - This is for the Women     28

Su Zi - Jealous Appeal     30

Patricia Carragon - Caution     33
(inspired by The Killers)

Vera Sirota - Instructions from Janine     34
Dedicated to Beat feminist poet Janine Pommy Vega

R. Bremner - Medusa                                      35
(for Jean Ray)

Erine Leigh- Women Unite, However They Can               37

Melony Overton - The Crones                              38

Stasha Powell - Sanctuary                                39

Andrena Zawinski - At Pine Cove                          41

Doc Janning - Bhakti                                     42

Marieta Maglas - Rondeau Redoublé for Elizabeth          43
Rosemond Taylor

Patricia Martin - A Goddess' Body                        44

Bengt O Björklund - Goddess Poem                         46

Karen Warinsky - The Dash                                47

Darius Phelps - My Mother Is a Depressed Goddess         48

Ksenia Rychtycka - The Many Tales of Lybid               51

Jon Veilleux - Ode to Ruby Bridges                       53

Rikki Santer - I'm Probably Not                          54

Ms Til Kumari Sharma - Existential Goddess as            56
Woman Survival in Hardship of Life:

Tammi Truax - Daucus Carota                              60

Linda Bratcher Wlodyka - The Veil                        62

George Wallace - Rose of Demascus                        64

Mark Andrew Heathcote - It was painful for the entire world to let you go — 66

Jeff Weddle Ph.D. - Blessed Be — 68

Kelly Boyer Sagert - Sisters' Keeper — 69

Julian Matthews - Snake Stories — 71

Chris Dean - letters to a tattered bodhisattva — 74

Danielle Bennett - Peripheral Visionary — 76

Linda Rizzo - Tough Girls — 78

Margaret R. Sáraco - One of Many Secrets — 80

Jay Simpson - Frontwomen — 82

Marianne Tefft - Woman Life Freedom — 83

Deborah Ramos - I Am Poetry — 84

Michael Sindler - Mother's Circle — 85

Debbie Tosun Kilday - I Want To Be A Goddess — 86

Gregory Cioffi - Apotheosis — 87

Kim Acrylic - Nasty Woman — 88

Dr Santosh Bakaya - The Girl under the Mulberry Tree — 89

Kris Janvier - Diamonds Grow With The Old — 91

Amy Christine Matus  Of Our Mothers — 93

Lily Swarn - Gaj Gamini — 95

| | |
|---|---|
| A.S. Coomer - i'm writing you this from the kitchen | 96 |
| Bryan Franco - You Were More Than Everything | 98 |
| Claire Conroy - Call Me Daphne | 100 |
| J R (Judy) Turek - He Tells Me I'm a Goddess | 101 |
| Laura Grevel - 1939 Hollywood Ghosts Bow over Hattie's Shoes at the Remake of Her Oscar-Winning Day | 103 |
| Sheila Lowe-Burke - Goddess of Truth | 105 |
| Joe Kidd - Night Vision Of The Goddess Of Love | 107 |
| Dane Ince - Sorry Hungry Pasta | 109 |
| Chryssa Velissariou - You Haven't Changed at All | 111 |
| Merilee Johnson - Girl with Frond by Central Park Pond | 113 |
| Igor Pop Trajkov - Silver Spoons | 115 |
| Susanna Peremartoni - Charles Bukowski's Women | 117 |
| Anthony Policano - Lady of the Snowlands for Kim Darst, 2009 Iditarod musher | 120 |
| Diane Barker - Goddess in Blue Jeans | 122 |
| Norma Mahns - Sweat of Salt | 123 |
| Sandra Feen - Things Fall Short for my parents, Rae Grace and Vernon | 124 |

| | |
|---|---|
| Fin Hall - Fifty (For my daughter Janine on her birthday) | 126 |
| Larry Jaffe - Ode To Women Of Strength | 128 |
| Saeeda Akhtar - She Rises (A Tribute to Womanhood) | 130 |
| Jennifer Browne - It puts the heart in my chest on wings* after Sappho | 131 |
| Nhien Vuong - On the 7th Day She Rested | 132 |
| Christine Donofrio - The Golden Mama | 135 |
| Ron Myers - Signal Hopping | 136 |
| Catherine Katey Johnson - A Woman's Love | 137 |
| A.M. Hayden - Hugging Nun at the Sacre Coeur | 139 |
| RescuePoetix | Susan Justiniano - Title Machinations of Sacred Silence | 140 |
| Virginia Shreve - The Song is Fire; The Steps are Wind; Poem of the Girl Not Believed, but Not Defeated | 142 |
| Jayati Roy - A Divine Encounter | 143 |
| Barbara Shepherd - Wonder Woman | 147 |
| CR Montoya - Remembering RBG | 149 |
| Mary Eichhorn Fletcher - Edith | 151 |
| Chrysavgi Kapella-Papadimitrio - Through Woman Springs the Greatest! (Ancient Greek Maxim) | 154 |
| Paul Richmond - Goddess Hecate - heh·kuh·tee | 156 |

**Lesley Constable - Brave Women** 158

**Amb Dr. Priyanka Neogi - Role Of Women** 160

**David Henri - Venus** 161

**Roxanne Hoffman - Saltitos del Corazón, Otra Vez /** 162
**Little Skips of the Heart, Again**

## Trier Ward

### Isis is Unconquerable

Isis is unconquerable.
She chopped her husband up
and threw him in the river.
We never ask why,
because every woman has her reasons.
She flies on golden wings, undefeated.
She is carved in the oldest crypts of man.
I paint her skin mahogany,
because she has the nerve to be dark.
She was never white, or shy, or apologetic.
She flies on golden wings through the
endless deaths of time.


Trier Ward is a mother, poet, and scientist. She grew up as an Air Force brat living around the world, and now lives in Albuquerque, NM. She performs at several open mics in the area.Her other interests include the arts, social activism, and wildlife rehabilitation. She has had three collections of poetry published.

## Ron Whitehead

**Redemption**
for Jinn Bug

1
Among all my remaining choices,
the only one left
was surrender.

2
I was of many minds,
a river elm tree with many branches
in which cawed a murder of crows.

3
The crows danced
in the November winds.
They were directing me to my next move.

4
A woman and a man
can be one force
yet remain fully themselves.
It is possible.
How do I know?
The crows told me it is so.
I believe in and trust crows.

5
For many years I was certain,
certain that one way or another
I would find a way,
after failure after failure after failure,
to succeed.
I was certain of my inevitable success.

6
Ice covered the stained glass windows.
Sunlight glistened through.
The shadows of crows
refracted dark colors, to and fro,
onto my writing hermitage floor.
My tumultuous emotions
were thrown about by the shadows of crows,
barely discernible causes.

7
Oh you who know truth,
I surrender.
Please redeem my weary bones.
Reborn me.

8
I am trying to figure out your accent,
your precise yet foreign rhythms.
Are you British?
From New England?
I know the crows know.
I ask the crows..

9
When the crows departed,
having marked new epistemological boundaries,
I had my answers.

10
Despite your three dreams
I knew it would be difficult.
I had never encountered anyone
even remotely like you.

11
I was way beyond mesmerized.
I was at the vortex of
a completely profound change.
12

12
The river had altered its course.
The crows were no longer a murder.

13
It was high noon for two years.
Storm upon storm upon storm.
Lightning and thunder,
snow upon snow,
Avalanches.
From the limbs of the river birch
in the backyard,
the crows watched.

14
Twelve years have passed,
since those two years of storms.
Although we now live four blocks apart,
you at Barduin, me in my writing cottage,
through the long winter nights
and the hot summer days,
less negative, more positive,
less defensive, more vulnerable,
with open hearts we still rest
in each other's loving arms.
After all these years, redemption.
The crows grin.


**Ron Whitehead**, U.S. National Lifetime Beat Poet Laureate Poet, writer, editor, publisher, professor, scholar, activist, U.S. National Lifetime Beat Poet Laureate Ron Whitehead is the author of over 30 books and more than 40 albums. A UNESCO Europe Writer-in-Residence, his work has been translated into 20 languages. The Legend of Ron Whitehead, a feature length documentary on Ron's life and work, is now available for streaming on Amazon Prime Films Documentaries.

**Christen Lee**

**This Is Only the Beginning**

Dim lights frame the hospital room.
My breath catches on the hard linoleum
as a crushing wave encircles me,
squeezes the baby.

It's sterile, this room with metal carts
gloves and gowns
and my arm, it bites with needles
as another tube fills deep red

my red blood
my clenched fist
my splayed body on display
as the nurses point and probe
and announce,
"It's time."

"Push!"
The nurses bellow
as I grit my teeth and my body sinks
under a tsunami.
I surface for words,
"How's the baby?"

A calm hand mops my brow,
"You've got this."
I tremble,
"No, no, I can't…"
A soft voice,
"The baby's almost here."

Daylight strikes
the room now blinding,
searing like knives.
"A head! Black hair!"

I writhe and I gnash, I squall and I slump
like a towel wrung dry.
Chips of ice feed my parched tongue.

"Just one more push!"
So I gasp, bear down,
impound my insides like sheet metal

I weep and I curse
and I promise you the whole world.
Yes, things will get better, just wait—
some stories have brutal beginnings.

I howl and I bleed,
rip hidden seams
and pour my life force into you,
my son.

You,
whom I will forever
push toward life.

You,
whom I will forever
pull toward love.


**Christen Lee** is a family nurse practitioner in Cleveland, Ohio. Her writing has been featured in Dulcet Lit, Rue Scribe, The Write Launch, Aurora, Humans of the World, Sad Girls Club, Encephalon, In Parentheses, The Elevation Review, and Moot Point among others.

## Mikayla Cyr

### Skin Deep

I ain't been right for a little while now
But, I suppose only the past knows
of how wrong I've been before

They say hope is spoken in hushed airs
I've never breathed
Silken spiderwebs delicately laced
around the tongue like a whisper
trapped behind teeth
They only miss you when
your bones become a garden

But I know not of a hope
so fragile as this
I was built like a tombstone by
the kind that clings to skin by the nails
Spitting blood with each gasp
Sick in knots if only to hold a handful

They say the future ain't as bright
as it used to be
But this fizzling lightbulb in my fist
Broken glass buried skin deep
Burns a promise of tomorrow


**Mikayla Cyr** is a Portland, ME native with an affinity for nature and the arts, as well as a passion for poetry that's lived for decades.

## Binod Dawadi

## Woman

You are gift of God,
You love and care,
You have different forms of life,
You are beautiful and lovely,
You are woman,


No one could take your place,
You are sister, mother and grandmother,
You are a great,
My words can't praise you,
We love woman so much.


**Binod Dawadi,** a polymath from Kathmandu, Nepal, is a beacon of creativity, intellect, and activism. Armed with a master's degree in English, Dawadi wields the power of words to enact societal change. His journey as a writer, teacher, artist, photographer, model, and singer is a testament to his boundless passion and talent.

Dawadi's artistic endeavors transcend conventional boundaries. His digital paintings and photography capture the essence of his surroundings, while his literary works provide profound insights into the human condition. His commitment to social progress is palpable in every stroke of his brush and syllable of his pen.

Tajalla Qureshi

**Woman: The Goddess of Poetry**

The lyrics of her resonance,
the whispers of her magnificence,
softly allocates the vibrancy, velocity
and engaging variety
All great beings, all great writings
I sensorusly stumbles upon her brilliance
Brightness and soulful blazings
She is the thought that rightfully clicks
She is the expression that the poet licks
through a profound pleasure with her sensation
where often fragrance dwells for admiration
where swiftly the pen swings, the aura brings
She is the first letter of your poem, your perfection
that the canvas uncovers, the pen discovers
and magically the lines convey closure in lovers
Her loveliness evokes the beauty of utterances
her innocence chokes the dynamic of flutterences
She, the divine wine, the poet's enchanted encounter
her lavishing lips, her belonging beats, reflect the fond of her
her artistic compels, her lovely lashes, redress the moonlight
her blushy cheeks, her necklace around her neck, remain
the magical delights
her rings in her hands, her presence,
her undefined fragrance keeping the imagination alive
She is since your existence, your poetic birth, your unheard
hearth that drives
As you pour her imperfection, you keep her radiance survive
with your survive.


**Tajalla Qureshi** is a skillful poet, essayist, fiction writer, columnist, interviewer, illustrator and an incredible editor from Pakistan.

**Megha Sood**

**Homage to My Hair**
After Lucille Clifton

I

My hair, a stranger in a family
of thick luscious flowing tresses
born with thin, frail strands.
Bald spots mapping every inch of my puny skull.
They are my crowning glory now.
They stood the test of time in fashion trends
curling, perming, and whatnot.
They don't like to be dyed,
streaked, or colored at the roots.
They have the shine that will put
your judgmental eyes to shame.
They don't like to be tied in a knot or
put up high on a pedestal as a bun
braided, highlighted, or shoved
to one side.They have their own way.
Favorite parting: left or right, they decide.
My hair has a voice of its own
though frail and thin:
speaks volumes alone.

II

My hair knows no bounds
and is limitless.
They hold no shape or form.
like water—
molds, and morphs where they belong.
With kindness, and compassion,
teaches me to accept life
as it comes along.

III
My hair has its own space and moves unabashedly.
Dispensing slithering truths like Medusa
ready to bring down your vulture eyes
and forked tongue to shame.
They hold a code, a legacy, a lesson in them,
neatly braided by my granny soft hands
making trails of kindness.
Teaching that kindness
is a gesture of acceptance.
Like the puny sapling breaking
through the crumbling earth
as it finds hope,
and grows through pain.

**Megha Sood** is an award-winning Asian-American author, poet, editor, and literary activist from New Jersey. Literary Partner with "Life in Quarantine", at Stanford University. She has four award-winning poetry collections. She is a Four-Time State Level Winner for the NAMI NJ Dara Axelrod Poetry Award. Her 900+ works have been widely featured in print, online journals, public exhibits, and anthologies. Her co-edited anthology "The Medusa Project" and other works have been selected to be sent to the moon in three separate rocket missions in 2025 as part of the historical Lunar Codex Project in collaboration with NASA/SpaceX. Find her at https://linktr.ee/meghasood

**Belinda Subraman**

**Christmas in "Independent Living"**

My mother was never satisfied
always complaining.
Some trauma shaped her into OCD
with unceasing grasp for control.
We followed her esoteric rules or tried to
and were punished for not understanding
for breaking her imagination.

(She had been so deprived
it was hard for her to give.
I seem to have picked up
her screaming weight of the world.
A fear grips from nowhere
The brain needs serotonin.)

Her love was a lottery.
Once in so many days or weeks
we got a kindness instead of an order
just enough to keep us hoping.

(She had a "breakdown" when we were small
and was away for awhile.)

After moving to "independent living"
it took her awhile to see the good.
She has everything she needs close by:
help, food, friends and family
except me, 2,000 miles away.
We phone-visit often until her ears get sore.
She is 94.

My mother said she saw one of my hairs
stuck on the mini tree skirt
in the present I sent
at Christmas. She wasn't complaining.

She said she just left it there.
a little family DNA, a little hug from me.



**Belinda Subraman,** Texas Beat Poet Laureate 2023-2025, is currently working as Managing Editor for BeatLife magazine and editor/publisher for GAS: Poetry, Art and Music. She enjoys collaborating with other poets and artists and has published many of these collaborations on her YouTube channel. She also interviews Beat Poet Laureates for the BeatLife channel.

## Chivas Sandage

### Persephone's Tattoo

Spring's first vine
grew from her left ankle, unspooling
along blue veins toward her littlest toe.
A second vine arched
across her shin
and a third wrapped her calf.
She texted to tell me
the vines were shadows
of vines. She'd taken a photo
dreaming of a tattoo.
This is how the shadows
do not fade with dusk.
Imprinted, now,
on her perfect body
born of my body, spring—
her favorite season—
follows her every step.


**Chivas Sandage** won second place in the Nuclear Age Peace Foundation's 2022 Barbara Mandigo Kelly Peace Poetry Contest. She won the 2021 Claire Keyes Poetry Award for a group of eight poems.

Her poems have appeared in the Texas Observer, Salmagundi, Southern Humanities Review, Soundings East, and The Long Now, among others. She is the author of Hidden Drive (Antrim House), a finalist for the Foreword Book of the Year Award in poetry.

Since 2006, she's taught weekly women's writing workshops in the Northeast, and now on Zoom. Sandage lives with her wife in Goshen, Connecticut, and San Marcos, Texas.

## B. Elizabeth Beck

## Woman Rising

She lifts her spirit when first note
is launched, feeling lightening
spin circles around her soul,
yearning to connect vibrations
to heal her heart broken, still
beating in tune when breath
ignites electricity she remembers
every mistake, each choice,
all decisions lead to this moment

life forged by instinct, wisdom
gained, feelings hurt, imagination
inspired to be brave enough
to connect divine intervention
within human tissue, blood
pumping, heart strong, soul
not shattered, only cracked
enough to allow light to guide
her body to rise as she imagines
blue swirls surrounding her in love


**B. Elizabeth Beck** is the author of five collections of poetry and the Summer Tour Trilogy. Her debut collection of short stories is forthcoming by Accents Publishing spring of 2025. She is the founder of Teen Howl Poetry Series and Poetry at the Table in Lexington, Kentucky. For more information about Elizabeth: www.elizbeck.com.

**Dinara Orazbekova**

**Paradise under the feet of our mothers.**

When we are born
Our mother angel protects us from harm
No matter how old we are
She's the only one who never forgets us.

Mommy will hold us in her arms
and hide us under her wing,
She gives us hope and faith,
She brings happiness, comfort and joy to our home,
She warms us with love and care.

Paradise under the feet of our mothers,
And what's important is that our children don't forget
That they're all connected to her by the umbilical cord,
Oh, how many odes they've devoted to her in their lives.

The world and the universe are in her hands,
And her children will always be her favorite,
God hears her prayers in heaven,
The most beautiful woman in the world.


**Dinara Orazbekova (Dina Oraz)** - poet, writer, translator, presenter, journalist, actor, director, public figure, head of the creative association "AVANGARD", vice-president of the ICPD, vice-president of the International Chamber of Writers and Artists CIEZART (Spain) - Kazakhstan, International Peace Ambassador of the National newspaper, Dahka, Bangladesh, member of the "Union of Journalists of Kazakhstan", IACL Ambassador. Author of three children's books. The author's works have been translated into Tajik, Azerbaijani, English, Belarusian, Ukrainian, Latvian, Turkish, Kazakh, Kyrgyz, Italian, Arabic and Uzbek languages.

# Catherine Lee

## A Rap Upon The Queen's Attraction

A poem commemorating August 29:
occasion of your birthday, Dinah Washington,
must, of course, acknowledge some misfortune—
that natal day you share with Charlie Parker,
(who garners all the celebration airplay)
and that jazz of premature departure
(yours, accidental OD, from diet drugs and booze)

You, successor to the Empress (Bessie Smith)
and yourself The Queen,
a pioneer of equal opportunity—
    ask alto saxophonist Bert Etta Davis, your road show
"Ladybird"
    or Patty Bown or Melba Liston, your arrangers

To sing the blues you had to
BE the blues,
to write the blues
you sang
your SELF unsilenced
THAT is your success

Like those who adored you in your time
I hear between your lines
messages not even your accompanists suspected—
    conversations lovers only hear
    and that mere possibility . . .
    Sang you Miss D: "Ask Any Woman Who Knows"
    "The Man That Got Away"
    and still
    "What a Difference A Day Makes"

Dinah, here's my admiring jazz womanist
birthday gift to you
reworking of your

no longer sick 'n tired
sisterly refrain
"Ask Any Woman Who Knows"


**Catherine Lee** explores poetry's percussive jazz voice from San Antonio, Texas, USA. Lee's collaborative multimedia writing projects have appeared in print and online. In 2024, Lee finished "Maverick Secrets" which explores how 1950s-'60s American TV Westerns programmed us as children with negative attitudes about minorities and approval of openly carried firearms. Its dramatic script is available in print at Amazon https://a.co/d/aUawkKs > and as a Dramatic Reading video at this VIMEO link https://vimeo.com/1030553167. Find details about Lee here: http://events.getcreativesanantonio.com/artist/catherine-lee/

**Puma Perl**

**This is for the Women**

This is for the women
who sit at long white tables
Women who remember
one another's children
who celebrate together
without resentment
who mourn together
with compassion

This is for the women
who dream
Women who sing
Women who sit
and write and sing
Women who string beads
in blazing colors,
who transform bits of yarn
to warmth and love
Women who learn to
strum a guitar
play a piano
dance on two
Women behind the camera
Women in front of the camera
Women who don't stand still
This for the women
Who have shared their stories
and those who have listened
Women who understand
a plate of food served
in a building hallway
so their sons don't go hungry
Women whose children
have slipped away

who have held a dying parent
who have raised somebody's daughter
who have put a grandchild to sleep
Wondering where is her mother?

This is for the women
Who gather together
Who sit at long white tables
Who bring carefully wrapped gifts
Who shopped at the 99 cent store
This is for the women
Who spent five dollars
This is for the women
Who always ignore directions
Who forgot the time
Who brought a pumpkin pie
Who know the colors
of the chakras
Who hate war and
love a soldier
Who didn't come today
Who live only in our hearts
This is for the women
Who sit at long white tables
Remember children's names
Pray to many gods or none
Speak in different tongues
Share a November moment
This is for the women…


**Puma Perl,** poet, writer, performer, is author of five poetry collections and a 6th soon to be published. She is front woman and lyricist for The Puma Perl Band, a spoken word and rock n roll band, since 2012. She's received four journalism awards and the 2016 Acker Award for writing. In 2021, she curated and performed in four shows as part of the HOWL Happening! Artist in Residence program. She continues to perform throughout New York City.

# Su Zi

## Jealous Appeal

i met you in maternity
      your new son
      a susurrating swaddle
      asleep at your ankles
  because you stood
      all the time we were about
  you stood

yours were the long bones of your mother
      and in those lines
      were clear ancestry
   you stood
      as we opened the metal door
      to put our hands on your son,
      but perhaps
      the food was too rich
      yours was a lean athleticism
but on the third day
      you were surrounded by doctors

across the concrete aisle
      your son stood
      a dark tremble
      alone
and i went to the nurse
      herself a new mother
      with a sturdy boy of her own
i went to the nurse,
      June,
      blonde, big boned, probably once Amish
i went to the nurse
      She on one side of the mesh metal door
      and i
      eye to eye
      we stood

        and in a quiet midnight accepted the new child

we had come to have the habit
of sleeping on the memorial graves of the ancestors
during lunch
the quiet hour

i had been told you were down the hill
        and i went to see you
        during the quiet hour

        you stood
        alone in your concrete room
        looking through the barred window

        there was a brush next to the door
        and I slid the metal panel upon its track

        upon your regal shoulder
        i laid my hand

        upon your regal body
        i laid my hand

        you stood for me
        looking out of the barred window
        into a distance beyond time

upon the grave of your grandfather, i slept
        and passed the ginger shine of your father
        in the glow of any day's end

later years
        would see the fame
        of your last son
        valid in blood
        his own lines saluted

you would stand

until the doctor came
until the needle came

to lay you down.



**Su Zi** has been previously published in a number of Beat anthologies, including New Generations 2024, Border Beats and others.
Zoeglossia Fellow Book titles include Danke (Ethel 2024), Flux (between the highways 2024) Chirp (Hysterical Books 2019) and some dozen other titles.

**Caution**
(inspired by The Killers)


Birthday wishes died at midnight
when Cinderella ditched her prince.

Her blacktop beginnings saw tarot swords
march in threes, eights, nines, and tens.

By cathedral doors
cautionary tales took root.

By the promenade
a song rallied for change.

Under mandatory incognito, she fought for her sanity,
threw caution west of the bay.

As seagulls flew around her,
she raised her arms to the sun, lips in affirmation—

found freedom when the mask behind her mask
lost its grip, fell to the rocks below.


**Patricia Carragon** received a 2025 Best of the Net nomination for her haiku, "Cherry Blossoms" from Poets Wear Prada. She is the editor of the new online journal, Sense & Sensibility Haiku, and listed on the poet registry for The Haiku Foundation. She hosts Brownstone Poets and is the editor-in-chief of its annual anthology. Patricia lives in Brooklyn, NY.

# Vera Sirota

## Instructions from Janine
(Dedicated to Beat feminist poet Janine Pommy Vega)

Decide you're not here to appease the provincial. Conventions are chains, especially for women. Make freedom yours.

Scale mountains. Conquer continents – not by military force or incursion. Seek the divine feminine in every culture.

Demand an equal love, like Lilith. The worthy will salute your power, bring you a cup of tea while you're writing.

Stand with the marginalized – children, prisoners, migrant workers. Believe in their inherent talents and voices. Support them in putting pen to paper.

Speak truth to power. Bang your pots against war and oppression. Never be afraid to raise a ruckus for justice.

Worship the beauty of language. Find the melody in words. I leave this sacred task for you.

---

**Vera Sirota** serves as the Communications Associate for the Hoboken Historical Museum, where she works alongside Poet in Residence Danny Shot on poetry programming. She is the author of the chapbook We Bow To No One, published by Bottlecap Press in 2023. We Bow To No One was the 2024 Chapbook Winner of the Eric Hoffer Award and earned a First Horizon Award for superior work by debut authors. It is included in the Poets House Showcase in New York City. Vera lives in Hoboken, New Jersey.

## R. Bremner

**Medusa**
(for Jean Ray)

The swivel of your smile turned men to stone.
But it was not snakes in your hair,
it was the twang in your eyes
and the tangle of your lips
that damaged so many irreparably.
Nightblack hair coiled like a cobra
about to strike.

Yes, Cinnamon Girl,
you California Cowgirl in the Sand,
who migrated east and traipsed
the gritty Greenwich Village sidewalks
with your many conquests trailing behind,
waiting to fall at your feet at the
snap of your finger cymbals.
Did you enjoy your Royalty?
The Queen of Thompson Street,
your subjects prostrate before you!

I heard you once, at the
Phil Ochs Memorial Concert in 1976.
You strapped on your Stratocaster
and rolled the place
with an electric, electrifying version
of "Small Circle of Friends".
All the great performers –
Melanie, Pete Seeger, Odetta, Tom Rush,
Tim Hardin, Ramblin' Jack -
were aching to do that song,
but who could refuse the Queen?

I wish I had known you
in your Medusa days
but then

I'd be a pillar of stone now.

(Neil Young's songs "Cinnamon Girl" and "Cowgirl in the Sand" were written about Jean Ray, half of the folksinging duo Jim and Jean. Phil Ochs slept on her couch on Thompson Street for several months, and married her best friend when he couldn't have Jean. And she mesmerized just about every straight male in the West Village in the 1960s.)


**R. Bremner**
A four-time honoree in the Allen Ginsberg Awards, R. Bremner has been writing of incense, peppermints, and the color of time since the 1960s, in nine books/chapbooks, and hundreds oj journals and anthologies including Climate of Opinion: Sigmund Freud in Poetry, International Poetry Review, and seventeen jazz poems in Jerry Jazz Musician. His eBook Mirrors, from Grandview University, is available free of cost from the author.. Ron currently lives and writes in Northern New Jersey.

**Erine Leigh**

**Women Unite, However They Can**

I resonate with a certain demographic...
Creative, intelligent, even prophetic.
These clever people are almost always women
(Some with lucky access to their husbands' incomes).

Not that I gladly lean into cynicism...
Mixed with sincerest interest and gratitude
In the large view, we need support and attitude
To step forward into our unrealized dreams.

Attuned with an awareness of womens' healing...
I need their support and involvement to stay afloat,
Have worked for years to pay my monetary note.
Great teachers readied me for this reckoning day,

Before they lifted up and sadly passed away...
I pray for their spirits, everyday feel a presence.
They shared selfcare's importance and inner essence,
Knowing it is not a selfish self-love practice,

But forms of inspiration to find our axis...
I build offerings,
conduct rituals, meet you
Wherever you stand, I respectfully greet you,
Hopeful you can honor my much simpler space.

Together we adapt to political violence…
As our rights move forward, are again thrust back,
We are once again maliciously attacked
By the highest court and forces in our nation.

We have daughters, we must not give in to despair,
But remember the women who fought, because we care.

'**Erine Leigh** writes from Eastport, Maine, as the sun rises on the truth. She served as Beat Poet Laureate of NH. from 2021 to 2023.'

# Melony Overton

## Crones

I like being in the company of older women
The crones
Women who are comfortable in their flesh
Women who have wisdom in their bones
Women who won't take any guff and
none of that sassy mouth stuff
Women who are tough
But who bake and who create
Women who in their power
And with each footstep make
Mother Earth quake
Women who are strong
Women who get along
Women who pass the time
 With long conversation
 Women who belong to me, my family
Women with vision
Who are wrinkled around the eyes
Who tell the God's honest truth
Women who withstand the test of time
Tell me, what kind of woman are you?


**Melony Overton** is a lifelong writer, wife, mother, witch and Reiki Master from Texas. This former newspaper journalist turned English teacher now Life Skills teacher writes poems when the muse is ready. She is an aspiring novelist who has various ideas for books begun and others brewing all at once. She practices the healing arts and does energy work along with reading tarot/oracle cards, all of which is her passion.

## Stasha Powell

## Sanctuary

Frenzied energy, all around—
the city hums, a chaotic pulse,
but here I sit, like the eye of the storm,
calm, collected, untouchable.
I feel the buzz of bodies rushing,
but I'm free, baby,
finally free,
'cause I put me first—
and yeah, that's taboo in my family,
a sin for the shame-soaked.
But tell me,
how can healing be a crime?
Goddess. Queen. Scarlet Woman.
They sneer, but I own it.
Sacred mind, sacred body,
this temple is mine.
Once, my aura was a live wire,
sensitive, raw—
the world ate me alive.
But now?
Now I'm a sanctuary.
No keys for the unworthy,
no entry for thieves of my light.
Protection, peace,
grace,
it pours back into me,
finally.
Feel this:
new emotions roll in
like waves breaking on some distant shore.
I don't even know what to call them yet—
but they're real,
and I feel them.
Self-love,
I'm basking in it.

Reflections in the mirror that I don't flinch from,
truths that don't sting anymore.
I believe,
for the first time,
in me.




**Stasha Powell** is an Ohio (by way of SF) gothic poet and creative writer with a flair for the macabre. Her work often explores themes of darkness, transformation, and empowerment. Currently pursuing a degree in Creative Writing with a concentration in Poetry at SNHU, Stasha channels her unique perspective into powerful, emotionally resonant pieces. She writes under the pen name Stasha Strange and can be found at www.stashastrange.com

# Andrena Zawinski

## At Pine Cove

After trailing the wooded misty path
to the cove, feet sliding on wet sand downhill,
after watching abalone poachers rise,
wet suited from the waters with their sea troves,
we brave the climb back, steadying ourselves
on thick branches and each other.

Back to the inn's rickety writing table,
a pot of market soup-of-the-day waits
to be warmed, wedge of peppered cheese
and crusty baguette on the cutting board,
sweet port picked up on the way in on
ribboning S curves that carried us here.

We slip into our oversized cable knits,
sale priced at the local mercantile, settle into
the blustery night opening a door to the sky's
threat of storm, where we will remain inside
safe and dry. Just two women getting ready
for dinner in lodging near the sea,

getting ready to drift off to sleep, wrapped in
a sash of fog and the warmth of each other,
old dog at our feet already snoring under the table
where a vase hugs three stems of fragrant Stargazers,
musky heads tilted the way women stop to talk
along coastal garden trails, ears of the cove listening in.
"At Pine Cove" ©Andrena Zawinski 2021

**Andrena Zawinski's** poems have received praise for free verse, lyricism, spirituality, social concern and have appeared in Blue Collar Review, Caesura, Progressive Magazine, Rattle, and others with work online at Women's Voices for Change, Writing in a Woman's Voice, Verse Daily and elsewhere. Her fourth full-length collection of poetry is Born Under the Influence. Born and raised land-locked in Pittsburgh, PA where she made a lot of noise, she now lives quietly with her wife on Alameda Island in the San Francisco Bay Area.

## Doc Janning

## Bhakti

In the nakedness of your emotion
bedecked in sunset's gold
and waves of joyful jubilation
you are become
a goddess

Vesperal vestal dreams
draped in mazarine robes of Midnight
are scrawled on nubile folds of vellum
as crepuscular kisses charm the stars

Avaricious silence claims the day
and echoes of light dance
amid unquiet marvels of delight
across horizons of time and space

The infinite geometry of you

Becomes

**Doc Janning** is the 82 year-old Inaugural Poet Laureate of The City of South Euclid, Ohio, and Third Poet Laureate of Cuyahoga County, Ohio. He has had poems included in 36 anthologies and many other publications. His first book of poetry, "Before Today ∞ Beyond Tomorrow, Poems from the Multiverse", published by Venetian Spider Press in November 2023, includes two poems nominated for a Pushcart Prize.

**Marieta Maglas**

**Rondeau Redoublé for Elizabeth Rosemond Taylor**

Bigger than her roles, world-class, and violet-eyed,
For being the movie's most legendary star,
Elizabeth Rosemond Taylor was greatly portrayed,
With her dramatic spark, as an actress so far.

She knew from her mother that this art is awesome,
In aeternum keeping her shining star so tight,
Wanting to be all or nothing and to become
Bigger than her roles, world-class, and violet-eyed.

During filming National Velvet, she was hurt.
Her heart vibrated like a string of a guitar.
Instead of leaving, she tried her role to exert
For being the movie's most legendary star.

She believed in herself and had self-confidence.
An immaculate, unique talent she remained.
As having genius and a raised consciousness,
Elizabeth Rosemond Taylor was greatly portrayed.

Her sheer charisma meant " Cat on a Hot Tin Roof",
Ad Astra per aspera Taylor-megastar,
Playing in 'Who's Afraid of Virginia Woolf? '
With her dramatic spark, as an actress so far.

Important awards are mentioned in her memoir.
To act in 'Butterfield', she was persuaded.
She dreamt of having " A Place in the Sun"~ a star.
In Memoriam, her name is serenaded.
Bigger than her roles…

**Marieta Maglas** writes from France, where she lives and works. Her poems have been published in The MockingOwl, Roost, Lothlorien Journal, Verse-Virtual, Massticadores, Silver Birch Press, Sybaritic Press, Kingfisher Poetry, Oddville Press, Dashboard Horus, Coin-Operated Press, Mayari Literature, Synchronized Chaos, Al-Khemia Poetica, and PentaCat Press.

## Patricia Martin

## A Goddess' Body

Her body is universal, celestial
embodying the mysterious pull of the cosmos
the unwavering essence of the heavens

It cradles the cosmic glow of countless stars
of every age and temperature
blue white yellow orange red
basking in their own radiant glowing heat

The Goddess' body is terrestrial
her bones lovingly cup life from the sea
fragments of breathing coral
hard and protective for survival
but pliable and soft at their marrow core
undulating and spawning in the moonlight
moving her through time and space

There are myriad mystic gardens
eternally blossoming, living jewels,
decorating her full figure,
her essence

The crown of perception at her forehead
radiating the soft scent of jasmine
proclaiming forever
she is a gift from God

Daisy eyes flutter, open wide
with piercing innocence

Bittersweet at the throat speaks unapologetically
proclaiming only truths

At her heart
a perfect red rose gives endlessly,

embracing eternal love

Radiantly, a full-bloomed sunflower
warms her solar plexus with adoration

At her sacral chakra, the womb of the world,
a white lotus witnesses all that is honorable and noble

Sacred to Aphrodite, myrtle adorns her private sacred mound
where love, beauty, and devotion reside
and always will

In her natural glory
the Goddess reigns forever
alive with vital life forces
at one, always,
with all that is human
all that is holy,
all that is eternal and lasting

**PATRICIA MARTIN** State of Connecticut Beat Poet Laureate Patricia Martin is an author, poet, performer/actor, and freelance writer who has been featured at numerous venues, on radio and television, and published in various periodicals and anthologies. Member of the Authors Guild, the Nonfiction Authors Association, and the Connecticut Poetry Society, Martin is the author of six nonfiction books, In Venice I Could Sing (poetry collection), and Is Love So Fickle, (haiku chapbook. www.patriciamartin.com.

**Bengt O Björklund**

**Goddess Poem**

there are times
when you walk next to me
in loud silence
whispering of all storms
we have created
when I can hear your skin
bones and all
raging like an evening raga
furiously fighting
for a place among the gifted
the in solace talented
in grief baptized
just to be visible and alive
and I can hear the flow
of your hot intent
as if on a mission of hope
leaning hard against the wind
dropping all pretense
in facing the day
so full of scars and bad tissue
so impregnated
with dark eyes and gestures
of hollow hate and disgust
yes there are times
when you walk next to me
and our days
furiously fall like leaves
faster and faster


**Bengt O Björklund,** Sweden Beat Poet Laureate for life. A prolific poet since the seventies and a respected artist and a percussionist. Known for his many years in Turkish prisons. Called Erich in the movie Midnight Express.

# Karen Warinsky

## The Dash

Reflective vessels
we drift and dream
scrape char from the meat
stretch shrunken sweaters
wax scratched surfaces
moonlight bright.

Jugglers,
we toss our many hats
into the busy air
catch most before they fall.
Acrobats,
we run, spin, pivot,
deliver and fetch,
cars like go-carts
wind in our hair
wishes out the window.

One day
we'll get back to that book
feet up
snacks at our side,
but today we are Brigid, Freya, Hestia
protecting home and hearth,
fire in our hands
sparks of wisdom
strong as a silver birch.

**Karen Warinsky** published poetry in numerous anthologies, journals and online sites since 2011. She is the author of three collections: Gold in Autumn (2020) and Sunrise Ruby (2022 Human Error Publishing,) and Dining with War (2023 Alien Buddha Press,) is a 2023 Best of the Net nominee and a former finalist of the Montreal International Poetry Contest. Her newest book Beauty and Ashes will be published by Kelsay Books this summer. Warinsky coordinates Poets at Large, a group that performs spoken word in MA and CT. https://karenwarinskypoetry.wordpress.com

**Darius Phelps**

**My Mother Is a Depressed Goddess**

I
Under this
blazing Georgia
sun, I kneel
down to plant
peach roses
for my
mother.

Each morning,
I wake up
and tend to
her garden
as she
watches in
reverence

My silence
is between
your suffering.

Our generational
trauma will
forever be —
a shapeshifter.
the malice
in our
wonderland

II

There were no
blossoms in
our garden
Just shrubs,

dried out soil,
skulls from
the remains
of our
beloved.

I long for
a home
where my
loved ones
are present
&
not faded
memories
decaying
on the walls
waiting for
us to join
in line to
prepare for
the war in
hell where
our ancestors
await for
us to
confess to
the sins
we didn't
commit.

III

I plant
the seeds
to regrow
the garden
she burned
hoping the
fertilizer

known
as our love,
will lead her
to to thirst
no more.

Mother -
together
we will plant
the gardens
that will covet
our new
world

The spines of
my peach
colored roses
will forever
break for
you.

**Darius Phelps**
An educator, poet, spoken word artist, and activist located in New York, USA, Darius writes poems about grief, liberation, emancipation, reflection through the lens of a teacher of color and experiencing Black boy joy. He serves as Poetry co- editor for Matter and an Associate Editor for Tupelo Quarterly. His work and poems have appeared in the School Library Journal, NY English Record, NCTE English Journal, English Quarterly,Pearl Press Magazine, ëëN Magazine, and many more.

## Ksenia Rychtycka

## The Many Tales of Lybid

(Legend has it that the Lybid river was named after the only girl
among the four siblings who founded Kyiv. – Oksana Faryna, Kyiv Post)

Some said I was haughty
rejected royal suitors

cried day and night
tears birthing a river

Some said I was queen
in an ancient time –

those who begrudged my rule
blackened my name

penned curled letters
on birchbark

branded me
an unfaithful woman

Some said I was a gifted spinner –
townspeople lined up

eager for my fine linen
whitened by the sun

Some said I was a water priestess –
saved a family of hardworking merchants

summoned rain out of parched sky
doused unexpected fire

Truth blurs into legend
centuries pass -- ancestral songs

passed down to children
endure even wildfire

When I died
my soul – reborn

Look to the river
that still carries my name

Look for the white bird
soaring through sky

Heed my birdcall
of impending floods

Look for me in spring's rainbow –
the best of omens



**Ksenia Rychtycka** lives in Michigan. Her poetry chapbook "A Sky Full of Wings" won the 2022 Eric Hoffer Book Award and the 2022 Best Book Award (American Book Fest) in the Poetry Chapbook categories. Recent work has appeared in The Poetry Distillery, Wordpeace, Peninsula Poets, The Literary Bohemian, Fusion Magazine and the anthologies: Shattered – Artists Inspired by Artists, Ukrainian American Poets Respond, and The Power of the Feminine I. Ksenia has traveled through twelve countries in Europe and lived in Kyiv, Ukraine, during the early years of the post-Soviet era.

## Jon Veilleux

### Ode to Ruby Bridges

She walked in grace
In little black shoes
Her mere presence
An anathema
To the hateful white faces
Screaming obscenities
At
Her little black face


**Jon Veilleux** is a retired Mainframe System Engineer who has written many poems and several short stories. He travels between Connecticut and Florida and loves the beach and searching for sharks teeth.

# Rikki Santer

## I'm Probably Not

what you're looking for,
my panties drawer crammed
with random
monogrammed hankies
that I shoplift from
thrift stores and on days
off I like to draw mustaches
with permanent marker
on all the honey
bear bottles at coffee
shops around town
and yep I keep a diary of quotes
from my favorite sardonic
TV judges and with my
morning prune juice smoothie
I relish watching footage loops
of fireworks, you know the kind
that look like it's raining spermatozoa
and I'm serious when I tell you
that I would have your favorite
knock-knock joke tattooed
around my left wrist to answer
the right one, so as I am two
people behind you waiting
for the carousel, I am transmitting
thought waves into your cranium
so that you will choose swan
boat and I will mount palomino
behind you and when

the sparkling music begins
we will twirl and twirl as
if we are riding in our very own
snow globe and we will suck
our clouds of cotton candy
until our brains melt and
leak right out of our ears.

**Rikki Santer**
In 2023, Rikki Santer was named Ohio Poet of the Year. Her forthcoming collection, Shepherd's Hour, won the Paul Nemser Book Prize from Lily Poetry Review Books. Please contact her through her website, https://rikkisanter.com.

## Ms Til Kumari Sharma

## Existential Goddess as Woman Survival in Hardship of Life:

The harmony of endurance is planted. Rd
The power of revolution to secure her ethics is her bravery.
The struggle of ethical existence is heroism.
She is not only hero but rewarded as creative hero.
She is brave to bring her sunshine in wisdom.
So she is goddess of purity and harmony.
She is fighter and warrior in the battlefield.
She is the glory of all human existence.
But today the moral woman is made as subject of joy and joke.
She is made as a working machine.
She should be loyal like slave to accept patriarchal norms.
She is identified with father, brother, husband and son.
Her identity is made inferior and arrogant.
But her struggle of existence is not praised by anyone.
She is not viewed as goddess of glory by few monsters.
If we are loyal, we have fear of using.
So we should be bold and brave.
The woman goddess is favored by nature but not by politics and so-called arrogant society.
If the woman is not in kitchen, people talk badly.
If I do not clean room, home and kitchen,
Next group criticizes me.
I am not owner of sweeper.
I am owner of wisdom and leading.
I am owner of my identity.
So I am goddess of existential sublimity.
Woman is the holy spirit of sublimity.
She is the quality of her ethics.
So she is supreme goddess.
She is supreme power to change world.
She is justice keeper or giver.
Woman beauty stands in ethics.

Her walk is like movement of the earth.
Her journey is to have genuine rationality.
Woman as goddess of purity and ethics brings
the essence of humanity.
She loves only brotherhood and sisterhood relation.
The beauty inside of mind leads whole earth.
So she is primary essence of living existence.
But we are identified with patriarchy in this society.
Why is our identity in destruction?
Why is woman seen as beautiful object only?
Why is woman seen as object of touch
from teenager male to aging males?
This patriarchy enters in her physical fitness only.
So she should be warrior to kill touching system of lust,
passion and negativity.
So the goddess quality is in inner rational and ethical
strength.
If we women do not know to make cooking,
sweeping cleaning and washing,
We are viewed as evil and monster like figures.
Is that right?
Is there justice?
Is she evil when she walks or runs
with sound against injustice?
So the quality of goddess is good moral ethics of humanity.
So respect the ethical woman with moral sound.
Treat her as your mother and sister.
Do not see her as joyful object only to view & touch her.
Respect her good doings.
The woman is the source of survival for all.
She is the glory of home, nation and world.
She is ethical existence.
The shining existence is in her good character.
Then she is glorified.
The woman is origin in existential beauty.
The beauty is highlighted within the ethical formation.
The shining lamp is in the ethical character.
The earthly decoration is designed by the woman essence.
The woman is the character of ethics.

The idea is the moral theme of society.
Woman is strength of the society.
The fraud women who have engaged in physical joy only can not achieve the ethical beauty.
I saw few women have engaged as with many males' joy to them.
That is woman exploitation.
So woman should be existed as ethical being with self-standing in moral is real light of goddess.
The woman virtue is in revolution against injustice and exploitation.
We women are goddesses when we can win against injustice and misuse to our soul and body.
So heroic soul & mind should be with us.
Self-awareness is our theme of life.
Then women seem as goddesses.
The woman spirit should have magic against the talkative and villainy actions to us.
We should be flames of fire against our misrepresentation.
We should be lighting to look forward who misrepresent to us.
The woman purity is undead.
The creativity is alive.
Heroic deed is flowering around world.
That is significant portion of life.
She is mother/sister to share as friend to sons/brothers.
The world must be decorated only with ethical women and men..
Woman art is glorified in her victory as goddess.
The woman empowerment can change the world when mind leads ethically.
Woman should be supreme power to change the universe.
The feministic rationality in ethics brings quality of goddess.
The strength of woman is infinite when wisdom of her self-awareness works a lot.
She is goddess of higher moral.
She is strength of extreme wisdom to lead all.
So she is highest glory when she has goddess quality.

Woman is the weapon of confidence.
She is ethical warrior to save her soul and body.
She is real fairy of every home.
Her emotion is wise.
Her logic meets scientific truth.
She is rational being.
She is supreme living entity.
She is real goddess of discipline.
So she is respected enough in the world
as goddess of purity.

**Ms Til Kumari Sharma** is a Multi Award Winner in writing from an international area from Paiyun 7- Hile Parbat, Nepal. She is known as Pushpa. She is a featured-poet and a best-selling co-author too. She is a poet & co-organizer of the World Record Book " HYPERPOEM". She is one of many artists to break a participant record to write a poem about the Eiffel Tower of France. She has got "World Creative Hero" award from LOANI: Leaders of All Nations International.
Social Network:
WhatsApp:+9779843910147/9749497960
Email: authortilks@gmail.com
www.pushpaism/tilaism blogspot.com

**Tammi J. Truax**

**Daucus Carota**

At Pleasant Hill Preserve
under the Emerson Elm
the Queen Anne's Lace
performs a dainty dance
to the muted music
of a slow summer breeze.

The flower's name, a fairy tale;
Queen Anne, a fine tatter,
one day pricked herself,
and a drop of her blood
plopped upon her lace,
leaving a purpled floret
in the center of a flower.

Fiction at its finest,
for Queen Anne's Lace
is actually a workhorse.
A commoner called Wild Carrot.
She's a host plant for the
black swallowtail butterfly
and a variety of aphids.

Her prodigious seeds feed
the ring-necked pheasant and pine mouse.
Roaming rabbits and white-tailed deer
stop by to enjoy a few nibbles
of her fresh flower and fern.
Her fluffy foliage provides the preferred
building material for nesting starlings.

And now, in my America,
I suspect, I fear
our sisters, our daughters
will harvest the maiden's lace,

as women have done in
the uncivilized before-times,
from India to Appalachia,
as an abortifacient.

Taken the morning after,
the Queen's seeds chewed
or crushed into a tea or slurry,
swallowed with greater doses
of desperation and prayer.

The real life maidens wait
for the purplish droplet to come,
for her womb to imitate the flower,
for whom, without patriarchal control,
as the seeds ripen, the blossom
curls inward to form a tight nest shape,
turns a brownish color, in an act

of self-preservation,
of self-protection,
of survival.

*Previously published

**Tammi J Truax,**
author of  For to See the Elephant and The Pearl of Portsmouth
https://www.instagram.com/tammi.truax/
https://www.goodreads.com/author/show/7234947.Tammi_Truax

## Linda Bratcher Wlodyka

## The Veil

A garment passed down through generations, sustenance for life, lies within a copper urn. Beatrice the chosen one, stands outside in tall grass. A veil drapes over her head hangs to her ankles, its intricate weave- flowers, winged insects, birds, veil worn to celebrate the coming of Spring.

Honey bees, hummingbirds, dragonflies, fly under the veil, alight on her face distribute pollen while the veil mysteriously emits a fine mist to accompany pollinating process. This ritual continues for six hours winged creatures come and go, are replaced by new swarms. Beatrice appears entranced, enraptured, yet solemn, except for her eyes.

Her eyelashes, lids, are heavy-laden with pollen, honey comb.
Her eyes rapidly swirl allowing the ritual to continue. The veil covered in yellow pollen, drapes heavily like a velvet robe. Winged creatures flutter, kiss her cheeks before exiting. Once the ritual finishes she unveils, lies on her back in the grass

intoxicated by her role as goddess of the meadow, garden, grass.
The veil will not attract visitors unless Beatrice is shrouded. Hours pass, she arises walks to creek drinks handfuls of water,
washes her face. Pollen and honeycomb rinse into the stream.
The veil is placed within the copper urn.

When the high tides return and the Blue Moon shows itself, the ritual is repeated. Earth's sacred, ragged plain cries out to the veil which elicits a signal to Beatrice disciple of Gaia, Goddess of Earth.

**Linda Bratcher Wlodyka** is the current Beat Poet Laureate of Massachusetts (2023-2025). Her latest publication is, If Brambles Were Bookends Collected Poems published by Human Error Publishing (2023). Linda is a member of the Florence Poet's Society and serves on their editing committee for their yearly anthology Silkworm. In October 2024 she attended "Lowell Celebrates Jack Kerouac" as a guest poet and speaker on behalf of NBPF.

## George Wallace

## Rose Of Damascus

she had a recipe
 for pain
  that knew
no boundaries
 an appetite
   for larceny
 a taste for
french poetry
   a pocket knife
  to puncture
    bourgeois expectations

she was possessed
 by parlor light
  and dark angels
she had
 a list
  of lovers
    long as a
peacock feather
 she wore
 marigold attar
  and cashmere

her intimacies
 were maddening
  her affairs
theatrical
 and her lips
   to me
  were copper penny
boulevards
 her voice

   was rain on cobblestones
and I,
   I was infatuated
with her hands


**George Wallace** (b.1949 NY, USA), Writer in residence, Walt Whitman Birthplace. Author of 42 chapbooks and 5 spoken word albums in US, UK, Italy, Greece, Macedonia, Portugal, Saudi Arabia, India, Spain. Major international poetry festival prizes and appearances, inc. Orpheus Prize (BG); Alexander Prize, Aristotle Medal (GR); Silk Road Prize, Poet of the Year (CN); Naim Frasheri Laureateship (MK); Corona d'Oro (AL); Naji Naaman Literary Prize (LB), Medellin (CO, Ledbury (GB), Lyric Recovery/Carnegie Hall (US). National Beat/Next Generation Beat Poet (US); Honorary Doctorate, CiESART/Royal Academy 2024 (SP).

## Mark Andrew Heathcote

### It was painful for the entire world to let you go

You sometimes held it all together.
Other times you were wreckage disparaged.

You were a flickering beauty. Marilyn Monroe
You were an orphan about to become a legend.
You were an actress about to take to the stage.
And star on a Broadway strip, in your early 20s

Fledgeling--wings sitting on a ledge, waving to the crowds
A figure of beauty, of innocents holding hands with Mowgli
You were kissing a serpent snake wondering
What's your fate? What is next? What's more to be done?

You were an orphan sailing the Egyptian Nile.
Where Moses was throwing roses
Or was it tablets of stone at your feet?
And Jesus said, do not throw your pearls before pigs.

You were an Aran lily dancing in the flames.
Wearing a swirling white dress, a sweet and tender rose
Little more than an orphan kid, I guess.
While some applauded and others loudly hissed.

Roles in The Asphalt Jungle, All About Eve,
Gentlemen Prefer Blondes, who could resist
This glamorous actress, this sex symbol,
This comedic 'blonde bombshell'
With an IQ attributed to be around 165
Only slightly less than Einstein.
She lived and died by her fix.
Hard living and barbiturates.

Lord, she sometimes held it all together.
Other times she was a wreckage disparaged.
She was a flickering beauty, a goddess Marilyn Monroe
It was painful for the entire world to let you go.

**Mark Andrew Heathcote** is an adult learning difficulties support worker. His poems have been published in journals, magazines, and anthologies online and in print. He is from Manchester and resides in the UK. Mark is the author of "In Perpetuity" and "Back on Earth," two books of poems published by Creative Talents Unleashed.

## Jeff Weddle Ph.D.

### Blessed Be

Being no one in particular,
maybe I am an angel.
Or maybe that's you.
I used to see
a very old woman of great radiance
walking through my town
and always felt enlarged
in her presence.
Being no one in particular,
maybe she was God.
She never looked in my direction
and I'm not sure I could have
stood under her gaze
longer than a blink.
It's been years since I last saw her
and now the world has gone to hell.
Maybe that's a coincidence.
But maybe I am an angel
and there is still hope.
I don't know.
More likely, the angel is you.


**Jeff Weddle,** Ph.D.
School of Library and Information Studies
The University of Alabama
Tel: (205) 348-4990
Fax: (205) 348-3746

# Kelly Boyer Sagert

## Sisters' Keeper

Am I not my sisters' keeper? As we
shout when wolves crouch down, and
hold back blood and tooth and claw
with flimsy skirts and petticoats
and when we cheer the jungle king
that lies with calves in sweet green clover
water washing rocks and mistakes clean.
Wisdom, pain and sorrow, shame
water washing rocks and mistakes clean.
Am I not my sisters' keeper
as the pressures of our lives erupt?
Who can calm my sister down?
Bowls of water, cool fresh water
wiping fevered brows with prayer.
Rock of Ages, cool fresh water
offering faith and love and hope and prayer.
Sensing spirits in the wind, women
open arms and gather in,
honoring, remembering truth.
Am I not my sisters' keeper? Speak
the name of Frances Ellen Watkins Harper
poet, abolitionist, I speak
the name of Emma Caldwell Gatewood
climbing mountains, seeking heaven.
Women clenching stories in their thighs,
and in their breasts and in their wrists.
Standing tall in unity, the
sisters reach for stars while wiping mud
from faces, boots and fingers, toes
Am I not my sisters' keeper?
Shout the words you tell 'em sister
knowing that they've said them first.
Oh, they are their sisters' keepers
midwives, gardeners, mothers, saints, oh
keeping secrets of the night, my sisters

hold them in their throats and hearts.
Voiceless women with a voice so strong
the Milky Way bends down in awe.
So shout it sister, say it loud
oh say it proud 'cuz am I not my sisters'
keeper as we dance in darkness, light
a lamp and hold that flame above hunched
heads? Candles flicker, hearts can break
while sisters whisper, sigh and moan and cry.
Leaving hearth behind, surrendering
what's safe, the sisters plunge
into the dark, burning fingers, scorching palms
and then they light that lamp again.
Then, oh my sisters.
Then, my sisters.
Oh, my sisters.
And then we light that lamp again.


**Kelly Boyer Sagert** is a freelance writer and poet living in Lorain, Ohio, thirty miles west of Cleveland. She loves to write about strong women throughout history, serving as the scriptwriter of the Emmy Award-nominated documentary, Trail Magic: The Grandma Gatewood Story and the scriptwriter and an associate producer of the new film, Victoria Woodhull: Shattering Glass Ceilings that is a nominee for the Toronto International Women Film Festival 2025.

## Julian Matthews

## Snake Stories

1

My mother had a relationship with a snake. I don't say this lightly or in jest. She really believed in it. Once, when I came home to inform her I was getting married, she said the "pahm-bu", in Tamil, had already visited and told her the news. Similarly, when we were expecting our first child, she already knew — the snake had delivered the message. I never questioned it.

When I was 13, we lived in a row of terrace houses that had an abandoned area behind that was covered in undergrowth, which attracted all sorts of creepy crawlies to the extended back kitchen. One day, we discovered a black cobra had made its home in a hole next to the drainpipe in mum's kitchen. I remember the drama of coaxing it out with hot water, with each of us armed with something: a bat, broomstick, changkul (hoe) and parang (machete) ready to strike, and screaming as it slid out and raised its hooded head, and somehow all of us missed the target, until my mother stepped in and sliced it clean through. She was always decisive that way. Never showed fear. Made me suck it up when I came crying from a fall or a cut, and sending me off, amid the snot and tears, to go get the plaster and Mercurochrome myself from the medicine cabinet. She did hug and show deep affection, like most mothers, but only when I was little. But I sensed immediately she regretted killing the cobra. She was Hindu by birth and converted to Catholicism when she married dad. The killing of a snake, even watching it being killed, is a bad omen. She must have made amends later, as is the custom, to future snakes that showed up.I don't remember her ever killing another, so the snake or snakes that came after must have come, delivered the message, and left in peace. I never knew whether the snake delivered only good news though. She would never tell us, anyway, if it were bad news.

2

Sometime later, there was a local story which made world news of a rubber tapper being squeezed to death by a huge python. Another man had stumbled upon the scene when the snake was in mid-swallow, its mouth stuck around the shoulder blades. It literally had bitten off more than it could chew. And it was later killed. My dad read the story out loud to us with a mixture of awe and sly humour. Of course, later there was a consult with the pink 4D book with the fierce Chinese god in front that had tiny drawings which corresponded with four-digit numbers. You looked up a drawing, usually if it came to you in a dream, and tried your luck at the Empat Nombor Ekor (four-digit lottery betting) shops. I don't think the snake number brought dad any luck, no matter how many combinations of it he tried. Just like the unlucky, hapless tapper who couldn't be revived.

3

My mother has passed on for over eight years now. The other day, my wife had a vivid dream of her which she remembered. She said my mum was hugging me tightly, something we rarely did when I turned adult. I wondered then whether there were snakes in heaven. And whether one came to her again, sending us a message through a dream. Maybe it was good news, maybe it was bad. We know mothers, and all dogs, as a matter of principle are sent to heaven when they pass. But what about snakes? Is there a place even for them there too? Years ago, when I told the story of Adam and Eve to my children, I thought after the fall, that the snake, logically, had to follow them out of Eden. Who would the snake torment or tempt in Paradise left by itself?

No snake is an island.

And I wondered about all the snakes in my life, the reptilian, and the two-legged kind. Whether it was worth forgiving and reaching out, or just moving on without the drama, without the need to assuage and make amends. Maybe it's the uncoiling of these times that has left some of us spiralling into apathy: less serpent, more servient. Some days, I have enough snake in me to swallow me whole. Most days, I just want to curl up, and be left alone. And then it occurred to me, maybe there was never a snake in my mother's back kitchen after all. She just used the story to remind me that there is a bit of snake in all of us. Sometimes, the snake in us makes us hiss, bite, tempt or torment others. Sometimes, it can constrict or wind us up. Maybe, to move forward all we need to do is make the choice to shed old skins and be remade anew. Maybe, the snake is just here to be the bearer of the message — the lesson from all this death and dying — and like my mother, we need to make peace with it and let it go. Maybe, we just need to listen to the sound of our own rattle and find our way back to Eden: and never, ever again kill the messenger.

**Julian Matthews** is a mixed-minorities poet from Malaysia. He is published in The American Journal of Poetry, Beltway Poetry Quarterly, Lothlorien Poetry Journal, Live Encounters and New Verse News, among other journals and anthologies. Link: https://linktr.ee/julianmatthews

# Chris Dean

## letters to a tattered bodhisattva

Dear Janine,
today I needed your conviction.
Voices for people may whisper
quieter than self,
but the echo in the vacuum
is glue that remains.

Dear Janine,
today you were the reminder
of the tattered Bodhisattva,
the duty of the Babushka,
and the bonds of sister and brotherhood
our humanity is meant to share.

Dear Janine,
today I cried for the world,
tears of grief and anger,
while your words washed
and held me
as the sobs shook my soul.

Dear Janine,
today tears flowed,
fell wet on the page
and a piece of you whispered,
"The work of love will never
be too much to bear."

Dear Janine,
today I rose as you lifted
with a tender strength of heart,
foot in front of foot, hand over hand,
to reach for others to hold
as your words held me.

**Chris Dean,** writes from the heart of Indiana. Their work has been featured online, in print anthologies and they are the author of two books of poetry, Tales From a Broken Girl and We're All Stories in the End, published by Storeylines Press

# Danielle Bennett

## Peripheral Visionary

He stands in awe of the figure in the close distance.
Time is constant, but in this moment, it shifts and bends to her will.
Its seems with every lift of her arm, sway of her hips, hand to her chest,
she's in control of the impossible.
The Arbiter
The Master of time
and anything constant.

He's okay with that, in fact, a willing participant, totally spell-bound by her
timeless beauty. He moves but without the same authority she has.

He thinks if only she were to turn to her right ever so slightly, she'd see love-
she'd see future-she'd see friendship and understanding,

She tilts her head in genuine way
Making her smile and eyes really mean what they say
to each person lucky enough to be in the way
ff her countenance.

HE knows its magical even though he only gets the definition of her perfectly structured right jaw line,
the almond corner of her right eye.
A profile to envy.

Then, suddenly
A moment he could not have anticipated.
With no one greeting her, still she smiles,
touches her shoulder to catch
the shawl that adorns her side

looks down at the half empty wine glass before her
looks up and gracefully moves her head to the right
just a quarter.
 He gasps.
She sees me at last!
He wonders
maybe love and future will manifest.
He moves from her periphery.
She, to her visionary.
An encounter that could be pleasantry
Or –the beginnings of everything.

**Danielle McGugins Bennett** born in Brooklyn, NY, now resides in Clifton, New Jersey with her husband and two children. She graduated from University of Maryland in College Park  Phi Beta Kappa and magna cum laude, earning a Bachelor of Science degree and Master of Science degree in education in 2002 and 2003, respectively. In 2013 she earned a second master's degree in Journalism from Columbia University and subsequently, became a published, freelance writer. Today, Ms. Bennett works with a variety of student populations, primarily on a high school level, as a teacher in the following subject areas: English, History, and Spanish.

**Linda Rizzo**

**Tough Girls**

Tough girls with
a chip on
their shoulders
and chipped
polish manicures
walking and talking
with soothsaying
hip swaying swagger
that grabs
the boys
like a love potion
of perpetual
motion and madness

Tough girls wearing
that black leather
whether they're
hot or cold
happy or sad
sexed up
or going down
to the Lower East
side by side
thoroughly eye-linered
and false-lashed
not abashed
at their own
axis bold as
love behavior

Tough girls wielding
their tower
of power to
the people
showing everything

they've got
stripped to the
bare-assed
naked ambition
to get some
recognition
and maybe it's
not too much
but just enough
to be
a tough girl




**Linda Rizzo** is a designer, a DJ, a photographer, and perhaps a Jedi. She is also an occasional writer and has had her work included in two of Pamela Des Barres' memoir writing anthologies. Having had various creative careers, she is apparently entirely right-brained. Linda is a native New Yorker, who still resides there, and considers herself to be a tough girl.

**Margaret R. Sáraco**

**One of Many Secrets**

We sit at the table, 2 cups of espresso
And an uneaten croissant to share between us.
I sip coffee.

"There's something to tell," I say, and wonder why I want to.
She already knows so much about me, but this…
Maybe it is because I don't want the secret to die with me.
While it is not something I am proud of, I am not ashamed
but it is a secret I hold in my chest.

Some people know. Those close to me back then.
I was only 18, and a scattering of others.
Once I told a friend, and, well, let's say we are no longer
friends.

My knees grow weak when I think of her expression.
Disgust. I remember. She was disgusted.
I didn't bother telling her the rest of the story.
There are reasons we do things, but I didn't go on.

Life is not a straight trajectory, and I was in love.
Well, here goes,
I drop it before us, right next to the croissant.

We sit in silence. Unusual for us.
I ask the waiter for 2 glasses of water
Just for something to do, fill the space
I am not thirsty. She breathes, looks at me
but doesn't react like my distant friend.

"Tell me about it," she says.
I do, and she assembles the pieces.
"I was a wild woman," I say.

Parts of me still wish to still be like that.
"It is a long time ago," she says. "Why did you tell me?"
"I'm not sure." In case you ever found out when I was gone, I think.
Dead, I mean. No one knows the entire story, except me.
"Can I tell it to you?"

"Of course," she says,
putting her phone in her bag.
"I am listening."




**Margaret R. Sáraco** published two poetry collections, If There Is No Wind and Even the Dog Was Quiet (Human Error Publishing) which was a finalist in the Eyelands Book Awards contest. She and filmmaker Bobe Wu won first prize in the Moving Words competition for their collaboration on "Dear Rorschach." Margaret was a semifinalist in the Laura Boss Narrative Book Awards contest, has received Honorable Mentions in the Allen Ginsberg Poetry contests and a Pushcart Prize nomination.

**Jay Simpson**

**Frontwomen**

Frontwomen sit at the back of the page studying the lines the societal plague

imprinted beauty's indelible construct patent effective at birth

mapped out processes to follow believe typed in bold's alarming content

concurrent life sentences subvert acceptance disturb encroaching thought

dissenting proposal questionable formula indelicate irony tears up the stage

powdered faces blurred identity potent nightlight's failed vision

useless parades endless chanting protests falter at the border

the line up scorches the mic ignites the band demolishes the room

take on the system defy the law fatality by default


**Jay Simpson** lives in Perth Western Australia. Recently published in Chewers by Masticadores, New Generation Beats 2024 Anthology, Lothlorien Poetry Journal, Cajun Mutt Press and Alien Buddha Press. Jay is the featured writer, both nationally and internationally in a number of online magazines and journals. Jay loves poetry, art, music, satire and black comedy. She is the Creative Director and Author at her blog 'livingdangerously',

**Marianne Tefft**

**Woman Life Freedom**

I am only one small child in a clan of women
Who have preserved all we know
Since the beginning of time
In the way we move our hands and hips
And the path our hair carves through the breeze
In other times and more forgiving places
My sisters freed their fingers of rings
That bind them in unquestionable subservience
And loosed their milk to flow at bus stops
Beaches and classrooms that welcome them
With my nieces and nephews in their arms
Yet still we fight for freedom and life
For even after thousands of journeys of the Moon
Since our prophets walked our hallowed hills
I am not yet my own when I leave my father's home
Or bring my howling legacy into the world
But only when my spirit folds my lifeless arms across my chest
And departs this plane for the last time


**Marianne Tefft** is a poet and voice-over reader who daylights as a Montessori teacher in Toronto, Canada. Her poems and short stories appear online, in print and on air in North America, Europe, Asia and the Caribbean. Her work has been nominated for Best of the Net and the Pushcart Prize. She is the author of Full Moon Fire: Spoken Songs of Love and Moonchild: Poems for Moon Lovers.

## Deborah Ramos

### I am poetry...

I am poetry.
I am timeless.
I am a woman.
I live in the crawl space
between breathing and ascending.
I am a map of my children. My grandchildren.

I am poetry.
I am the sacred feminine.
I am a woman who
always belongs to herself.
I wear silver braids of wisdom.
I creak. Parts fall off when I walk.

I am poetry.
I am water.
I am the wild woman
with a mermaid tail.
I cascade from one body to another.
I pour out of this world.




**Deborah Ramos,** a poet and artist, grew up in San Diego, California. She is the author of from the earthen drum of my body, and is currently working on her next collection. She writes about the sacred feminine, ancient affairs, roadkill and her cats. Deborah's poetry has appeared in many anthologies, and more. Deborah's creative life includes traveling, writing, exhibiting her art and photography, as well as hosting Poets at the Grove readings in Balboa Park, San Diego.

**Michael Sindler**

**Mother's Circle**

the women in my mother's circle
each, in different ways, my life nurtured
filled cracks in knowledge I could fall through
with confidential ears that I could talk to
about so many things I didn't understand
as I struggled on the road to be a man
in my heart, each one still holds a special place
their wisdom still echoes from beyond the grave
with their compassion and their empathy
those priceless gifts of time they gave to me



**Michael Sindler** is a Denver resident and a native of South Carolina.  His work crosses genres including poetry, fiction, non-fiction,  memoir, theatre, and songwriting. He has been published in a variety of national print and web venues. He has collaborated with and participated in a number of media bridging projects and productions with museums and arts organizations throughout Colorado. He has featured in and facilitated virtual (and IRL) poetry readings, performances, and workshops across the globe.

**Debbie Tosun Kilday**

**I want to be a Goddess**

I want to be a Goddess
A Beat Goddess
Following the path of the Beat Goddess Ruth Weiss
Or sharing my voice with passion
Like Diane DiPrima
Or maybe a outrider
Like Anne Waldman
All these women are Goddesses to me
Their writings have lasted through the years
But then when I think of it
I too am a Goddess
In my own way
And you are Goddesses too
Expressions of
Kindness
Empathy
&
Love
That's what being a Goddess means to me


**Deborah (Debbie) Tosun Kilday,** is the owner/CEO of the National Beat Poetry Foundation, Inc. based in Connecticut, USA along with its festivals: National & International Beat Poetry Festival, Kerouac Cafe, and Goddess Festival. She is also owner of New Generation Beat Publications, BeatLife Magazine, and Kilday Krafts. She is a next generation Beat Poet, award winning author, writer, nature photographer, and artist.

# Gregory Cioffi

## Apotheosis

I drop to piously kneel before you
Craving to enter your tangible temple
My resolutions I shall follow through
My only proposal: don't be gentle

You deem me worthy and invite me in
And demonstratively remove your bodice
I honor you with praises upon your skin
I'm entering an impeccable goddess

I break out, a fever dream hypnosis
Such unadulterated elation
I never considered apotheosis
But you just triggered deification

You took me to exaltedly enshrine
And have elevated me to the divine


**Gregory Cioffi** (SAG-AFTRA, AEA) is a professional actor, an award-winning director, professor, and published author. His debut novel The Devil in the Diamond was released in 2023 by Henry Gray Publishing. Many of his stories have been archived in numerous libraries including Yale University's Beinecke Collection (Rare Books and Manuscript Library). Greg is an Adjunct Professor of English at Long Island University, an Associate Professor of Literature & Composition at Post University, and he also teaches
Creative Writing, Poetry, and Basic Acting at Nassau Community College. http://www.gandeproductions.com/

## Kim Acrylic

### Nasty Woman

A nasty woman's hot pink fetus blooms, bursting into a smile beneath the vast, rainbow sun. She covers the scabs on her knees with sugar and glitter. Her glamour congeals against her anemic membrane. Portraits of inequality are reflected in her pupils, framed like a funhouse mirror.
She will rise.
Her monthly abductor colors outside the fragile lines of her upside-down, menstrual-tinted smile. The feminine dark passenger hitches a ride, only to strangle itself with the images that appear closer than they are in the rearview mirror.
She perseveres.
Choking on her bubblegum-flavored breath, the religions of men taint her promises with the bittersweet secrets of patriarchy. Her Sunday best exudes an euthanasia-scented perfume. Turpentine-stained lips kiss her prayers goodbye.
She is reborn.

**Kim Acrylic**, from Seattle, Washington, is an abstract artist and unconventional punk poet. She has been writing for over 30 years and has been featured in several anthologies. She also has two volumes of poetry available for purchase.

## Dr Santosh Bakaya

## The Girl under the Mulberry Tree

A cuddlesome child charms the sky
mouthing tongue- twisters under the
mulberry tree.
Magical mulberry mesmerizes.

Magical mulberry mesmerizes.
The ten- year old smiles
as a litany of words tumble forth from her mouth.
.
Happy, hearty hibiscus.

She daintily plucks a hibiscus flower,
and with a broad smile, puts it her plait.
Unadulterated joy spilling in her veins,
she again bursts into a lovely refrain.
Free.
Uncluttered.
Unburdened.

Her wild hair cascades down in riotous playfulness,
and she gasps at the tapestry of sparkling colors,
that the sun has magnanimously unleashed.
"Tippi Tippi Top. What colour do you want?"
Her friends are busy playing,
swaying to an inborn juvenile music,
yells of rambunctious joy fill the air .Oh boy!

She hops towards them, wanting to join in the fun,
wondering what colour she wants.
But the sun is soon covered with a grey cloud.
Loud- loud- loud - thumps her heart.
She hears a shout.

"What are you up to? Wasting time?
Girl, you are getting married soon.

Come and help me in the kitchen.
Don't you know, it's already noon?"

Her mother yells from the window of her thatched cottage.
The girl quickly removes the hibiscus flower from her plait,
and dashes home. What if she is late?
She shrugs off the quick- welling rancour,
waving ruefully to her playmate.

She passes the village pond on the way,
where village women sit exchanging gossip
about their in-laws.
Tittering, their teeth glittering in the noonday sun,
elaborately gesticulating and slyly whispering.
Is freedom frothing?
Unfazed by the echoing peals of laughter,
she dashes home, stopping in her tracks
to pick a displaced feather, forlorn.
Also a skeletal branch and stripping it of twigs
and little boughs, her ears pricked to the sloughing trees,
singing a dirge for displacement.
But a little away from home, she styles the branch into a crown,
picks up a pair of roses, and sticks them in the crown,
smilingly hopping into the house, ignoring her mom's fake frown.


**Dr Santosh Bakaya** of India, internationally acclaimed for her poetic biography of Mahatma Gandhi, Ballad of Bapu; biography of Martin Luther King Jr. is an academic, poet, essayist, columnist, novelist, biographer, TEDx speaker, and creative writing mentor, whose TEDx talk on the Myth of Writer's Block is very popular in creative writing Circles, and so is her weekly column Morning Meanderings in Learning and Creativity.com. She has thirty best selling books. Her latest book is Din about Chins.

## Kris Janvier

## Diamonds Grow With The Old

These liver spots has formed
a diamond shape on her neck.
She constantly feels the heat
of these leering eyes of people
peering at them
as she walks by,
which causes them to back away slowly.
Thus, her curiosity chronically escalate,
so as her confidence.
Her smirk deepens her dimple.

Refracted images of her
zooming in and out of
these diamond rings and bracelets
that were in display
behind tempered glass from Jared's.

In honor of her imperfections,
they sparkle through every single color
of the spectrum.
Raw and uncut,
these edges constantly move
by multiplying cells
that are known to contain
information,
but they themselves will soon
be stuck with the others
who travelled for a couple of months
spreading the good word to the new ones
that this Sista is as bright as
the light above her and them
and have warned that they will age like the
messenger before them,
but always leave out that their deaths

will be unnoticeably quick.

But after years of living near
the equator,
not a shred of qualm consume her
as she's on her 5th stage of grief.

As more northern people look on,
her laugh lines extends even more,
her gaze became sensual and relaxed;
her flip-flops vibrates higher,
high enough for the neighbors to hear
from 5 blocks away while she struts down
Main Street.
Everywhere she goes,
her youth remain
while these diamonds grow with the old…


**Kris Janvier** is a poet, actor and author from Baldwin, NY. He self-published his first book titled "Drift" in March 2024. "Drift 1.5" was released in December 2024. He's a member of the Multicultural Council of NY and The Scene. He has performed in local open mics for 7 years. His poems are published "Nassau County Voices in Verse 2023", "Nassau County Voices in Verse 2024" and other anthologies.

**Amy Christine Matus**

**Of Our Mothers**

Of our Mothers
is
one velvety jewelry box
 a single precious barrette
 two pearls
silver clip-on earrings
 the modest wedding
 band playing Waltzes and Cannons in Alpha as  our
ancestry and our legacy meet as Goddesses do
in lilac and foxglove
 Violet and crescent moonlight

since conception perceived itself we
of our Mothers and with Gaia animate
whose fluctuating dial have us
every age all of the time and very tightly loved we are so
loved by the familial bond born rocking alive in the arms of
our mothers wailing with alive
 as our crying refills spring of newly opened energy
harnessed only to be given name symbolic of our aftertones
we are swaddled in the same air every library on earth
breathes and we are told to run to play to learn of the
wisdom freedom carries

Of our mothers we are immortal together somewhere in
forever to stay
we are Of the Goddess of whose beauty marks and
freckled elbows we share exactly like those of gardens and
our mothers

turning selves to fireflies calling out " Hey! Look at me!" each
cartwheel in pool naturally asking the goddess to reflect
Shine Back
 while Of our mothers
we meet ourselves and each other
 and cheer.

**Amy Christine Matus** (Wisconsin Beat Poet Laureate 2020-2022) is a poet and artist from Milwaukee, WI who finds collaborative collections especially dear and is thankful to be included here. Amy is finishing a collection of poetry and short stories and much enjoys yoga and walking her dog, Hope.

# Lily Swarn

## Gaj Gamini

Is she the goddess from the ancient temple
Striding out from the sanctum sanctorum ?
Come alive in flesh and blood on this balmy night ?
The heavy scent of Indian incense
heady and tranquilizing
The voluptuous curves statuesque and alluring

Her Gajgamini steps halt outside a door
Cacophonous noises jar her delicate ears
The man laying in obeisance in front of her
Each morning with a silver salver of flowers and fruit
Violent and abusive with his docile wife

The Durga on a tiger sashays out of temples
Hurling aside the pedestals men place her on
Shaky, rickety with the weight of traditions
She demands her rightful slot in this world
Unfettered , uncrushed ,naturally divine

Love her like a gift not a victorious trophy
Treasure her tiny desires for she's worth much more
Her luminosity lights up your entire universe
Before she is a mother, sister, wife or daughter
She's a whole new being to be cherished for life

**Lily Swarn,** International Beat Poet Laureate from India ,and Caesar Valejo award for Literary Excellence. Lily Swarn, is an Internationally acclaimed, multilingual poet, author, columnist ,gold medalist ,university colour holder, radio show host ,Peace and Humanity Ambassador. She has authored 9 books and ,has 2 Chandigarh Sahitya Akademi awards besides The Panorama Golden Book Award Her poetry is translated in 21 languages and she has over 70 awards .Her book of Urdu ghazals , Yeh Na Thhi Hamaari Qismat is highly acclaimed.Her latest book getting recognised worldwide is A Bejewelled Tiara which has poems of love and peace.

# A.S. Coomer

## i'm writing you this from the kitchen

because i can't stop drooling over you
& there's a fresh roll of paper towels here

i'm writing you this from the kitchen
where i brush my teeth & strain
out the melodies to new songs
& your harmonies goo like grilled cheese
when i get it hot enough

i'm writing you this from the kitchen
because the light is better in the mornings
&, even in exhausted umbra,
there is such radiance in you
& we're here so often
you with the recipe
me: red-eyed
& a-grinning
cutting the butter

i'm writing you this from the kitchen
because things are getting hard—ain't it hard?
maybe i'm mining a vein better left
to greater gods & less fragile mountains
but the smells of cooking & you
feel too good to be true
& i only feel worthy of white castle

i'm writing you this from the kitchen
where i sit at your heels
a hellbent rain dog
just a-howling
eyes a-begging,
breath a fetid pant
& you feed me
like a stray

& like a stray
i've found my way
into your heart

though i'll chafe
i'll wear any collar
you put on me

don't bother
with the paper towels
why the waste?
i can dry my eyes
on the dishrag

**A.S. Coomer** is a writer & musician. He runs Lost, Long Gone Forgotten Records, a "record label" for poetry.

# Bryan Franco

## You Were More Than Everything

I never thought of you as a badass.
You were just Meemaw.
You were never just Meemaw.
When you were born in Bodrum, Turkey,
your given name was  Mazel Tov (good luck in Hebrew).

It's assumed you were around six when you emigrated
since no birth certificate or passport existed.
You and my grandfather were arranged before the boat left.
you married after you turned 18.

On your first day of school,
the teacher asked for your name;
another Jewish girl told you the teacher
would never say your name correctly.
She said: You can use my name Matilda
which became your legal name.

But everyone always called you Mazel Tov
except your closest friends who sometimes called you Hazel.
One day, when they were at your place playing Mah Jong,
the 1960's tv show Hazel was on in the background.
You said I wish my name sounded more American like Hazel.
Unlike al he other women in your circle who
were from Turkey, Rhodes, Italy and Egypt,
who spoke virtually perfect English,
your English was always a bit broken.

At your funeral, the rabbi mentioned
that you were a single mother.
I never thought of you as a single mother.
Single mothers, to me, were either divorced woman
or single women who had unplanned pregnancies.
My grandfather died when you both were in your forties.
My father and uncle were 5 and 12 respectively.

You were a single mother.
You were a tough disciplinarian.
You raised disciplined, smart, ambitious, successful sons.
They both served in the military before college
and accessed tuition through the GI Bill.

I never thought of you as poor.
Some people would say the small, cramped home
you and your sons lived in after your husband's death wasn't much,
but it was everything to me and my brothers.
I never saw it as small even when we moved from city to city
into homes that were at least 3 or 4 times larger.

You were more than Meemaw.
You were more than Mazel Tov.
You were more than a single mother.
You were more than everything you were.
You were a badass.



**Bryan Franco** is a neurodivergent, gay, Jewish poet from Brunswick, Maine. He is published in Australia, England, Germany, Holland, India, Ireland, Scotland, and the US. He was a finalist in the 2022 and the 2023 winner of the NAMI New Jersey Mental Health Poetry Contest and is a Pushcart and Best Of The Net nominee. He hosts Café Generalissimo open mic, and an artist and culinary genius. His book "Everything I Think Is All in My Mind" was published in 2021 by Read Or Green Books.

**Claire Conroy**

**Call Me Daphne**

I've been shot by the arrow of Eros.
Cupid's vengeful lead laden shaft pierced me,
A poison to protect my heart and mind
From any attentions of Apollo.
I am a mere wood nymph, not a Goddess.
Free and alone, smiling in the green breeze
With the wisdom of a clear topaz stone.
Like the Metamorphoses of Ovid,
Daphne in her worship of Artemis
Cloistered in an authentic sisterhood.
Answering the call of the wilderness,
Of waters, of clarity, harmony.
Unlike Daphne, I will no longer run
From the unwanted affection given.
I will stand in the river of myself
While my legs take root in the rocks below.
I will change my skin to the flesh of wood
To escape the grasp of lust and of pride.
I have now accepted my laurel wreath,
All alone, and you can call me Daphne.

**Claire Conroy**, Beat Poet Laureate of Maine 2024-2026, has self published two books of poetry ("Listen" in 2018 and "Silent" in 2022) and a chapbook ("Rumors From Dead Lips" in 2024). Born in Portsmouth, NH, she is a proud board member of the Portsmouth Poet Laureate Program and is the host of their open mic, The HOOT. Claire also hosts Beat Night and Shine Open Mic at Flourish in Biddeford, Maine; along with hosting Painting Poetry in Dover, NH. She is a featured reader on the Poetry Bus Tour 2025.

# J R (Judy) Turek

## He Tells Me I'm a Goddess

He tells me to look in the mirror
see my reflection as more than pretty
though I don't admit to that, and
he knows how I focus on the flaws,
imperfections and less than fine lines;
he traces his fingertip across my brow,
unfurrows worries I've been clutching
to smooth the path down my cheek,
across chin, circle up over down
my nose to linger on my lips. I tell him
I'm not young, don't sport a sleek bod,
have wrinkles everywhere. His finger
on my lips ceases my speech, shhh....

He tells me I'm a beauteous goddess,
my scars, invisible to everyone but me,
are earned from wars won and life
faced, lived, and loved. I tell him
he is blind to scaley skin on knees
and elbows, ghostly impressions
from stitches, sutures, puckers and
excess waist weight too kind to call
a muffin top.  He tells me I've ridden
roads tougher than me and come away
with scrapes and scratches to prove
my wins; have confronted growths
and joints weaker than my driving need
to succeed at all I attempt.  I tell him
it saddens me that my body sags
in all the wrong places, skin once soft
and supple has lost its elasticity, doesn't
glow without makeup to contour cheeks,
more bags beneath my eyes than Amtrak,
and he smiles, lets a little chuckle out
to soothe us both. He tells me I embody

fabulousness and I blush all over.

Eyes downcast, I tell him it's hard
to admit I've slowed down, can't keep up
with twenty-somethings as we race the day,
run errands, sweep through a supermarket,
get dinner going while running the washer
and vacuum as though a game show clock
is ticking off a win/lose contest. Pursed lips,
he tells me for the thousandth time that
these things don't matter much; we need
to pace ourselves, face obligations in priority
order, and hellfire knows no one has ever died
of dust so forget the fast-paced race and relax.
Eyes on his, I admit again, that he's right; he
is always and forever right for me.

He tells me after more than forty years,
I am still the young girl he fell in love with,
sees us growing into one another, learning,
loving, each day living and thriving, and
going to bed cuddled in dreams for more
of the same a thousand tomorrows ahead.
I tell him I hope he truly believes that and
planting his lips on mine, he tells me
in no words that he loves me just as I am.



**J R (Judy) Turek**, LIP&LR Poet-in-Residence 2024-2029, LI Fair Sup't of Poetry, 2020 Hometown Hero, 2019 LI Poet of the Year, NYS 2017 Woman of Distinction, Bards Laureate 2013-2015, 29 years as Moderator of the Farmingdale Creative Writing Group; 2 Pushcart nominations; editor, mentor, writing coach, author of 9 poetry books. She lives on Long Island with her soul-mate husband, Paul, her dogs, and her extensive shoe collection.  msjevus@optonline.net

**Laura Grevel**

**1939 Hollywood Ghosts Bow over Hattie's Shoes at the Remake of Her Oscar-Winning Day**

as Clark, Olivia and Vivien line up to see,
the fabulous actress arriving soon they hope.
Oh oh yes! There she is . . .

the Hattie McDaniel at her grand soirée!
Where servants hold her jacket of gold lamé,
where Hattie stands on stage
glittering in turquoise silk brocade.
She smiles her famous mile-long smile,
belts out ballads, jazz, and
"Dis, Dat, Deez, Dem, Dey"
that witty tell-all-how-it's-been,
while we all do sigh and tear up
and show her due respect

inviting Hattie to sit at our tables
and allow us just a minute
of her precious time.
And all have written poems
dedicated to this tower
of behavior, talent and endurance,
and then sing songs praising
Hattie as an example of how
our own children should grow.

There would be a dance and dear Hattie
would be Queen of the Ball
her dance card filled with eager beaus,
her feet swept off the dusty floor
and into clouds of dignity.

There would be a chance for all attending
to apologize for lack of couth, for barbarity,
and the unbelievable things they used to think,

and these pronounced with a becoming humility
to give assurance that a new world
had climbed upon the mountain,
and if not perfect, we would at least
try to be something like a person.


*Hattie McDaniel , (1893-1952), an actress, comedian and singer-songwriter, was the first Black American to win an Oscar. She won it for her role in the film Gone with the Wind(1939). She arrived at the Oscar ceremony only to find that she had to enter by the back door and could not sit at a table with whites. She wished to be buried in Hollywood Cemetery, but at the time of her death, that graveyard was reserved for whites only.


**Laura Grevel** originally from Texas, now lives in Austria. Laura is a performance poet, fiction writer and blogger. Her writings are eclectic, tackling the immigrant experience, human rights, narratives and nature. Her work has been published widely in anthologies, literary journals and online publications. Laura often reads and features online at international open mics and events.

**Sheila Lowe-Burke**

**Goddess of Truth**

Never really thinking of oneself
As beautiful, or even pretty
Surrounded by so many others

Such loving, lovely women
Sharing life's experience
Of expression and wonder.

One may ponder
The years passing by and sigh,
Longing for the wisdom of maturity

Present even then,
Constantly refining and honing,
Finally knowing

The collective brilliance
Clarity and loveliness
Can never dim

The tiniest whim
Of honest truth and lasting beauty
The meaningful support

The genuine smile
The warm embrace
Every lustrous, luscious trace

A faceted laser beam of
Diamond reflection
Focused as one

Singularity, yet in collection
Offering divine protection
Camaraderie, revelry

Joy, and ecstasy
The paradox and paradigm
Of goddess Individuality.



**Sheila Lowe-Burke,** DR.HC – Michigan Beat Poet Laureate 2024-2026, Official Poet – Govt. of Birland North Africa, 100K Poets For Change, Michigan Rock & Roll Hall of Fame. International touring, recording, author, poet, songwriter, recognized as one of 50 most memorable women of North America 2024. www.joekiddandsheilaburke.com

# Joe Kidd

## Night Vision Of The Goddess Of Love

Even when its hard to love, love with all that you might render
for this is what the world will see when you are no longer
here to speak of all the love you had to share and offer
but held within despite the pain of carrying such a burden alone
with all beloved souls aligned and caressing a common grief.

Born to grow with a heart of gold and diamonds that fall
from ruby lips, given every treasured smile, every accolade and praise
until a tear became a flood to wash away the haunting fear
that someone may not wish to hear the sound of love between
two worlds.

A castle filled with silver tongues beyond the limits of naked eyes
beneath the roar of glorious fury, thoughts erupting and spilling out
into the molten mind of destiny, a hand that clutches all that moves
and dwells upon volcanic soil to breed and sing and disappear.

Let it be to happen in peace, this fate awaits all men of
honor to clear the path and plant the seed for a future that
blindly follows suit, and remember every act that never
happened all the words that could not be spoken, then love
them all as the book is written the pages turned and the
cover closed.

The blood that flows into the chalice, the sacrifice that all
surrender, its value in a limitless realm is all the proof
that nature needs to find its twin, the super child that lies within

the mirrored shade of one who knows beyond all faith
and all belief
when flesh and bone falls and the spirit calls,
it is love that will rise
to answer all.



**Joe Kidd DR.HC** – Michigan Beat Poet Laureate 2022-2024, Official Poet – Govt. of Birland North Africa, 100K Poets For Change, Michigan Rock & Roll Hall of Fame. International touring, recording, author, poet, songwriter, fearless revolutionary artist/activist.
www.joekiddandsheilaburke.com

**Dane Ince**

**Sorry Hungry Pasta**

Oligarchy you say
I am sorry
I am hungry
Is that a pasta dish
I am hungry
Creamy Orecchiette
Is what I thought you said
I do not hear so well on my knees
In prayer
For wisdom
Will the goddess come
Lend me a riddle
To pick the lock of madness
To form this universe
In one instant
We wed this bloodshed
High up the orchid lives on air
Everywhere I look
the story shaded by destruction smoke
Reeks of wanting need
Waking from meditation
How many wives

How many husbands
Lost the 51 one pieces
Without a head
Daughter of a god
The god
And the stories told of the mighty and all
Are the stories of us
Us murdered by tongues
The lies find truth
Can you see it in the ripple in the pond
Reflecting you to you
Fully formed by your agency

The myth is that you are a god's idea
The idea of your father
In not a lasting blink
The coil of cold snakes
Probing within the darkness of humanity lost
But will you come anyway Minerva, Athena Shree
Marry this mortal
Thrown pot on the wheel
The stick pokes down
The obese son inflicts mindlessness
The outcome is unclear
From here we are going where
Anywhere anywhere
Leave me a riddle
To pick the lock of madness
Take my mortal feast
Is what I thought you said
I do not hear so well on my knees
Nothing stops the blooming


**Dane Ince** originally from Texas, resides in San Francisco, CA. Dane is an internationally published poet, hosts a weekly open mic "Time to Arrive," Beat Poet Laureate for California 2022-2024, and publisher at EYEPUBLISHEWE.COM

**Chryssa Velissariou**

**You Haven't Changed at All**

Someone with your name
reacted to my new hologram.

Suddenly, both suns—
burning high at their zenith—
flickered out.

Dizziness…

Ah! Is it lack of oxygen?
A bitter needle pricks my chest.
I stumble back.
For a moment, I hoped it was you,
that your heart ached too,
that you could not bear the absence.

I was wrong.
Some indifferent old man from my past spoke.
An old man—just as old as me.
"I have aged, yet my soul remains the same, as does everyone's,"
I answered into the microphone.
"Everyone whose love was hollowed to the bone,"
I thought, but did not say.

What am I waiting for?
I rage at myself for still waiting.
I rage that my heart betrays me,
that it refuses to forget.

Light-years away,
and still, your memory unsettles oblivion.
How is it possible?

Somewhere, beneath soft soil,
you rot back on the first Earth.
You never loved to travel—
not even to my home.
You never wanted eternity,
not even for your own poetry.

And me?
Tell me—
why do I resurrect you, again and again,
with such unbearable pain?

I dig, as if searching for an answer.
Nature always comforts me, even here.
And through my oxygen mask—
but the horizon is burning.
If I do not carve my lament into the void,
its fire will consume me whole.

I am nothing now
but an experiment drifting too far
for anything to touch me.

Except you.




**Chryssa Velissariou** from Greece is an award-winning poet, educator, and cultural entrepreneur. Honored for her educational project version of the Eratosthenes experiment (2011), she is also a Lifetime Beat Poet Laureate (National Beat Poetry Foundation, Inc.). She leads Erasmus+ projects, integrating theatre, cinema, and New Technologies into education, empowering youth and promoting sustainability.

**Merilee Johnson**

**Girl with Frond by Central Park Pond**

The young girl and I walk past the pond.
She twirls in her hand a frond.
Her other hand in mine is wet
from reaching into the pond to get
the attention of the ducks and geese.
They swim calmly as you please.
On the path, she spies a ring
and gasps in delight and starts to sing.
She tries it on her small finger.
I don't know whether we should linger
to see if the owner comes along.
I stroke her hair as she sings her song.
"You'd be sad if it were yours and you lost it.
Shall we wait for her? Just sit?"
She nods but is downcast on the bench,
playing with the ring she feels was meant
for her to wear, hers to keep.
If she gives it up, she'll no doubt weep.
Would losing it sooner bring her less pain?
I try again to explain.
"It must be something very dear
to the person who has lost it here.
Like your grandma's golden wedding band
passed down from her mother, worn on her hand."

Twenty years later: "Aunt Debra," she says,
showing me her diamond, soon to be wed.
"I'm reminded of that day in the park---
we just went there on a lark---
and I found a ring and started to sing,
and the sound an older woman did bring
looking for the ring, its loss her fear.
When she saw I held it, she erupted in tears.

'You found it!' she cried with pure happiness.
'Oh, this ring I'd really miss.
On our wedding day, my husband gave me this.
We had fifty years of wedded bliss.'"

Now I say, "You wanted it so.
But you smiled at her and let it go."
Caroline beams and takes my hand.
"I couldn't keep her wedding band.
To her, it meant so much more.
This, I just couldn't ignore.
She showed me what had been inscribed
on the ring's inner side.
It felt good to restore her ring to her finger,
and it was you who helped that lesson to linger."

My eyes shone with joy at this wonderful being
who'd turned out so well, not my first time at seeing
her generous spirit, her loving heart.
And to think I might have played a part.



**Marilee Johnson** is a New Yorker aspiring comedian but still has one foot in the poetry and writing community. Her children's book The Boy Who Caught the Moon was published by Mayari Literature, and her poems, short fiction, and monologues have been included in anthologies. She participates in various open mics, both online and onstage. She earned an MFA in Creative Writing at The New School.

# Igor Pop Trajkov

## Silver Spoons

We are fed with baby mashes by them
under our pillows are hidden
the surfaces are shiny, washed
in mirrored hopes, which
according to French customs
should bring many bene-
fits to us.
Till reaching 6 my sister used to collect them
by her governess taught- the one
with French training, elegance
bourgeois, with a discreet smile
but who never smiles.
Nevertheless she is not allowed to
she would be immediately fired from work
also if she suddenly sits down
it would be like she's to herself
contradicting
she taught the children
that this is how armchairs get destroyed
that is why we should sit down slowly.
And I, the older sister, collected 6- now I have a whole set.

And I really think that both of us
have been well served by luck
we have received everything we needed
we are now tied to the family mangers
our children receive them
the silver spoons that flatter.
We have never struggled much
the spoons have meant a lot to us
and will mean a lot to those whose children do not struggle
in the cycle of rebirth
are fertilized by self-purification
and the cessation of fear
from the domain of uncertainty.

**Igor Pop Trajkov** from Republic of North Macedonia has published a lot of poetry, prose and theory, receiving many international prizes and acknowledgements. He is an editor of books and magazines, being one of the most productive authors in the region of SE Europe. He is also a visual artist, film author and playwright. Igor Pop Trajkov recently received his PhD in cultural studies.

## Susanna Peremartoni

## Charles Bukowski's Women

hey, Henry Chinaski,
Charles Bukowski's Women


hey, Henry Chinaski,
where were you yesterday,
flirting perhaps
with divas of smoke-filled pubs?

the hookers have no feelings left
maybe one more cigarette is their only personal request
in addition to the service offered.

your constant struggle on emotionless
nights mixed with the scent of sluts,
whispers smelling of alcohol, minutes purchased,
your weakness, your desperate struggle
with a flesh and blood blonde, brunette, black concept, that's
all you have left.
blue panties, tight female curves bitten in the TV light

hey! -

"you boys can keep your virgins
give me hot old women in high heels
with asses that forgot to get old"

women—proper women—are terrifying
they all want your soul, even though you try to keep what's
left of it in a depraved world.

when did you really feel good
at the moment
you penetrated a wet,

warm, big-breasted hot stuff.

there is nothing left between you and the idyll
at the bottom of your glass, between women's legs,
nothing harmonizes with you.
You must fight and suffer for joy until the end of your road.
You must earn it, that's how it's worth something, Mr.
Bukowski.

The soul wants to expand; it is thirsty for adventure, strives
for new forms.
Now I think
the soul of Mr. Bukowski moved on to other guys
where were you yesterday,
flirting perhaps
with divas of smoke-filled pubs?

the hookers have no feelings left
maybe one more cigarette is their only personal request
in addition to the service offered.

your constant struggle on emotionless
nights mixed with the scent of sluts,
whispers smelling of alcohol, minutes purchased,
your weakness, your desperate struggle
with a flesh and blood blonde, brunette, black concept, that's
all you have left.
blue panties, tight female curves bitten in the TV light

hey! -

"you boys can keep your virgins
give me hot old women in high heels
with asses that forgot to get old"

women—proper women—are terrifying
they all want your soul, even though you try to keep what's
left of it in a depraved world.

when did you really feel good
at the moment
you penetrated a wet,
warm, big-breasted hot stuff.

there is nothing left between you and the idyll
at the bottom of your glass, between women's legs,
nothing harmonizes with you.
You must fight and suffer for joy until the end of your road.
You must earn it, that's how it's worth something, Mr. Bukowski.

The soul wants to expand; it is thirsty for adventure,
strives for new forms.
Now I think
the soul of Mr. Bukowski moved on to other guys


**Susanna Peremartoni** was born in Hungary and completed her schooling there. At the age of 23, she moved to Germany, where she lived and worked as a ceramic artist up to 7 years . She currently lives in Budapest, Hungary. She is published in English, Italian, Australian, Canadian, and American literary magazines. She was a jazz poetry CD producer and has produced several podcast broadcasts. She also engages in photography. Her last exhibition was in Vienna.

# Anthony Policano

## Lady of the Snowlands

for Kim Darst, 2009 Iditarod musher

Aching and anxious
awakening in snow blind rapture
wrapped in layers of North Face gear
caked in overnight ice
with all of the mandatory equipment in tow;
sleeping bag, ax, veterinary notebook,
shrink-wrapped dog food, dog-food cooker for
melting snow for water
memories of New Jersey summer shores never
cross your mind
Oh my goggle-eyed lady of the snowlands
hungrier than a husky
too numb for loneliness or regrets
racing for the love of sixteen canines
racing to keep in shape
racing to replace the soul stealing games
the sports channels promote in the lower 48
racing to escape the epidemic of
New Jersey shopping-mall madness
racing like a bride to her blizzard wedding
spirit betrothed to sixteen dogs and wild country
racing for a cup of steaming coffee
in a wall-papered kitchen
racing for the aroma of baked apple pie
and a good shot of bourbon
racing for a spot of fleeting fame
on the front page of the Anchorage Daily News
racing to stay human
racing to prove a woman's worth
is measured by her passion
racing to prove a woman's grit
can ignite a man's to cinders
My Dearest Kim Darst

I wish I were there on that copter
airlifting you out of danger
halfway to glory on your virgin run
half of the 1,131 miles
you wished you could have finished
half of Nome to Anchorage
half an Iditarod is still pretty damned righteous
Oh My Dearest Kim
I wish I was the pilot greeting you
in that far distant place
of sudden whiteouts, moose and grizzly
rescuing you as you disqualified yourself from
the competition
when you called for help for your lead dog Cotton
his temperature dropping
his hypothermic eyes-rolling
I want you to know that your selfless exploits
rescued me from office cubicle walls
and mind-numbing meetings
from inner fears that kept me chained
to a mush team of my own making
pay raises my trail markers
retirement my finish line
How I wish I was there to greet you
with outstretched arms
handing you blankets and a dry expedition jacket
hugging and warming you until
you were so hot and bothered you'd
shove me off like one of your beloved huskies
who just got too carried away

**Anthony Policano** is an Italian American poet and photographer, born in Brooklyn and raised in Queens and Long Island. He is a board member of the LI Poetry Collective (LIPC) and the LI Poetry &Literary Repository. He was editor of a Walt Whitman Birthplace publication. Anthony's poems are published. He has one book of poetry.

## Diane Barker

## Goddess in Blue Jeans

A modern-day Diana
I move through concrete jungles
illuminated by city lights
Exchange silver bow for shopping bags
Hunt bargains not woodland creatures

I am Diana
Fleet-footed not with laced-up sandals
but worn-out sneakers stained with urban grime
Golden tunic and floral hair ribbon
now headphones and tank top

I am Diana
Quiver swapped for laptop bag
Technology bridge time and space
Oracles no longer provide answers
Alexa Google Artificial Intelligence

I am Diana
Close friendships forged by life experience
Present-day nymphs sharing laughter and tears
Confidences whispered in the breeze
Rooftop bar's neon replace moonlight

I am Diana
Namesake of a triple deity
Holding true the spirit of protector
Contemporary façade illusive
I am the goddess in blue jeans

**Diane Barker** began her writing journey in response to empty nest syndrome. She became a member of the Farmingdale Library Creative Writing Workshop, celebrating her 21st anniversary with the group. She is an award-winning poet and has been published in several anthologies. She resides in New York with her three goldfish and four snails.

## Norma Mahns

## Sweat of Salt

Purple Chrysanthemums
Each summer day, blossom
Not work, women's play
Her heavy shearing
To "glen and gather"
The paddle her tool
To travel, where
Praise the woman
With righteous hands
Purple Chrysanthemums
She dare not look back
Perpetually propelling
Her faith forward with shears
She straddles, her kayak
Her tool her paddle
She dare not look back
Forward fleet of bare feet
Disembark simultaneously
With sweat of power
And stability
Sharing Purple Chrysanthemums
Her friendship holy
As savory salt
In the righteous woman
God finds no fault.


**Norma Mahns** currently lives in Pocahontas Arkansas.
Her poems have been published in several collections, and underground papers.
She has a chap book of poems titled "Paper Plague."

## Sandra Feen

## Things Fall Short
(for my parents, Rae Grace and Vernon)

Tap shoes first, before shoelaces.
Ballet slippers second, on a Monroe, Connecticut
toddler names Rae Grace.  She teaches dance
in Bridgeport, in her teens. A redhead: 36-24-26,
her model digits. Her goal:
become a Broadway Radio City Rockette.

In 1953, she takes the Brown Train Trolley
to the Showplace of the Nation, asks
to perform all routines first, show perfect
precision, flawless kicks, but
dancers must be no shorter than 5'6,
and measurements taken in stocking feet.
Rae peeks 5'3, so she

resorts to plan B, the thorough lesson
her daddy Raymond taught her,
and in her 1950 Studebaker Champion
shifts gears to an extreme: picks
Columbus, Ohio on a map, takes her
typing, shorthand, and skills both
obstinate and resilient, to this
random Midwest city.

She finds immediate employment:
head secretary at Columbus' west side
Hilltop psychiatric clinic, then

rents a women's boarding house room
a mile from work, on Ogden Avenue.
Another woman arrives at the same hour
looking to rent, but was short
the amount of money for down payment,
so Rae Grace offers to room with her, split

the cost of a slightly bigger one with twin beds.
Kathleen, grateful for Rae's generous proffer,
insists on setting her up on a blind date
with her boyfriend's 6'4 blond-haired
blue-eyed football player buddy
in return. It's a deal, Rae laughs.

That Saturday night, doorbell rings.
Rae Grace peers through peephole,
views top of a brown crew cut, like
grass dulled and singed after flames.
She opens the door to a man with
brown eyes to match, much shorter,
assumes he is a wayward stranger
but he says her name.
Polite inquiry responds:
Are you a college football player?
He says he plays baseball for the Otterbein Cardinals.
I'm Vernon, he says.
How tall are you? She dares to ask, still not letting him in.
There is a short pause.
I'm 5'6. How tall are you?
There is a long pause, long as a train home
from Broadway to Bridgeport.
5'3, she whispers, looking down at her feet,
then slight midget of a pause, from Vernon,
before he states: That's a very nice height,
and his brown eyes grin into her blue.
She opens the door wide.

Two years later, they return to Monroe's November,
marry at the Congregational Church
where she was member, and had
her first dance lesson.

**Sandra Feen** was the 2022-2024 Ohio Beat Poet Laureate. Her fourth collection is a collaboration with Cliff Treyens, called There's a Rock on Martin Avenue, and is published by Venetian Spider Press in 2025.

**Fin Hall**

**Fifty**
(For my daughter Janine on her birthday)

So, you're 50.
Think your nifty
Well I've been there before you
And it doesn't  hurt
Your knees hurt
Your back hurts
Your head hurts
Maybe your stomach  hurts
Even you eyes and ears may hurt
But being  50 doesn't hurt.
It's everything else that might
Right?

You always were smiling,
Blue eyes beguiling in every photo
Laughing,
Not pouting as is the modern trend.
Except in one. When you were being a surly adolescent,
Not wanting to wear a hat in the cold and wet,
Sulking when I put a hood on you
To keep you dry,
But your young, glowering face
Looked out of place.
Even in the wind and rain.
Ooh the pain.

That time you fell in the mud,
With a squelch
rather that a thud
On the way to meet your new child minder,
Playing a blinder in your Sunday best,
Now a mess.
Bit it was ok
We went back another day

It was the same one that lost you
In the big shop
You weren't really lost,
Just you were short and couldn't see over the top
Of the counter
And round and round yous went
One side and the other
It wasn't really a bother as you were found.
As you can see,
Still smiling.

And then you changed your name from Hall to Rae
With all your kids,
Surprised you are not grey.
Well, we never know ,
Since you change the colour so many times.
That's fine,
It shows you don't stand still.
Well you didn't, but since your knees hurt…


So, here you are aging disgracefully
And I wouldn't have it any other way
Where the follies of youth
Helped you find the truth in who you are.
A star no matter what anyone says
A mouthy star, but a star no less,
But I wouldn't have it any other way,
Still my Princess.


**Fin Hall,** was born and lives in North East Scotland. He is current International Beat Poet Laureate. He is a producer, filmmaker, published and performance poet, book reviewer, publisher and facilitator.

**Larry Jaffe**

**ODE TO WOMEN OF STRENGTH**

Aesthetic waves
emergence of spirit
form beauty modest
feminine inspiration
riding strong
she is her own Galahad.

A ripped cape
A flight of nuns

Tears shimmer from eyes
in joy not sadness
obstacles of life
overcome
leaving her mark
in the universe.

The mirror gasps

WOMAN IN BLACK
The storm rode the wind hard
Bacchanal restored at
outpost wild.

There she stood
eyes direct

dumbfounding passerby
in a depreciating wilderness

never before could such beauty
be assumed

Eyes smoldering foils of victory

Moon shallow witness
hiding in blackest shadow

She is the woman
who makes dreams.

I SEE WOMAN
I see woman
the corners
the curves
the smiles
and disturbs

I see woman
the painting
the canvas
the brush
the universe

I see woman
the warrior
the mother
the saint
the lover

I see woman
I see you


**Larry Jaffe,** Lifetime Beat Poet Laureate lives in Florida with his wife Shelley. He is an internationally known and award-winning writer, author and poet. For his entire professional career, Jaffe has been using his art to promote human rights.

**Saeeda Akhtar**

**She Rises**
(A Tribute to Womanhood)

She walks through storms with quiet grace,
Her heart a lantern, a glowing space.
With every scar, she learns to shine,
A tale of strength in every line.

She sows the seeds of dreams untold,
Turns dust to pearls, weaves sand to gold.
Her hands may cradle, build, or mend,
Yet never break, they only bend.

Her voice, a river—soft yet strong,
A hymn of love, a warrior's song.
She carries worlds upon her spine,
Yet greets the dawn with eyes that shine.

She is the flame that lights the way,
The moon that guides, the dawn of day.
Unshaken by the winds that blow,
She rises still—she will not bow.


**Saeeda Akhtar** is a renowned poetess from Lahore, Pakistan. Her works have been widely published and earned prestigious accolades, including the Kazi Nazrul Islam Literary Award. She actively contributes to global literary forums, bridging cultures through her poetry and powerful expressions. Her words resonate with readers worldwide.

**Jennifer Browne**

**It puts the heart in my chest on wings***
**after Sappho**

I wake, wondering for
whom he whirrs. When
there is no click-reply, I
pause, wait again, look
through the window at
an empty branch. You,
loveliest, dear one, even
this dark morning, are a
silence-holding moment.
I sing, I sing. There's no
other I hear speaking.


*title and golden shovel on a line from Fragment 31 ["He seems to me equal to gods"]


**Jennifer Browne** falls in love easily with other people's dogs. She is the author of American Crow (Beltway Editions, 2024) and the poetry chapbooks Before: After (Pure Sleeze Press, 2025), In a Period of Absence, a Lake (Origami Poems Project, 2025), whisper song (tiny wren publishing, 2023) and The Salt of the Geologic World (Bottlecap Press, 2023). Find her in Frostburg, MD and at linktr.ee/jenniferabrowne.

# Nhien Vuong

## On the 7th Day She Rested

When people ask me
what will I do
with all this time
with myself and away

I tell them, truthfully,
I am not going anywhere
I don't need to leave. In fact
I am learning how to stay.

I am sitting in bed, flirting with fresh
ideas of a more fecund and feral faith
ideologies of blanket fertility
male and female and gender-fluid issue
that glance on me like every morning's rays
through cheap white blinds.

I am batting tiny black lashes curled upward in hope
held perfectly upturned by yesterday's waterproof mascara
my hot-mess hair hanging to mid back and black and netted
and nestled in
fabricated down pillows
unabashedly finding them
better than the real thing
(it's the truth).

These minted manicured fingers of every woman
take their time
fondling ancient truths
untempered by time and
buried inside
the encrusted curves of a primordial seabed

I am rounded by this pain and
legions of liquid shame
all my female ancestors
[no stanza break]
are holding their breath, cramping
underwater
wondering whether the eggs
inside us can hatch
all on their own.

(Mother Mary did it. Why can't we?)

Stories of ecstatic union sweep over me
and now, Beloved,
I am taking both our hands
I am pressing them together, in anjali mudra,
(which Christians call "prayer hands")
and I am repenting again and again,
surrendering
to our former enemy–

the Silence.

Shh.
Our Mother and her mother and their mothers
do not say a word
and I understand their intentions now
and I give
in.

When people ask
What will She teach us now
after all this time away
I take my time and

I do not breathe
a word.

**Nhien Vuong**

Born in Vietnam and raised in California, Nhien Vuong is a Stanford Law attorney turned Unity minister. A contemplative Enneagram thought leader and community builder, Nhien is the founder of Evolving Enneagram, a community-centered organization whose mission is to offer spiritually inclusive, Enneagram-informed compassionate spaces for transforming lives. Nhien mentors individuals from diverse backgrounds around the world, helping people to awaken so they can live more fully from their divine nature. Nhien is the author of the upcoming book, The Enneagram of the Soul: A 40-day Spiritual Companion for the 9 Types (Hampton Roads, April 7, 2025).

## Christine Donofrio
## The Golden Mama

She stands in the doorway and just gazes
At her offspring and then moves closely near
Her capabilities of sensing are in full force
She sees the beauty in her children
One of a poet the other a designer
She teaches her daughter to do artwork with colorful
crayons to empathize the beauty in the ugly world
she came to know.
The colors stand out and help pave the way for her children.
Her golden years are right in front of her and she wants to
leave the world better than she found it.


**Christine Donofrio** is a published poet and creative writer from Cleveland, Ohio. While in college she worked on a Feminist Journal called Femspec. Christine loves crafts, her cat Lily, and painting in her free time.

**Ron Myers**

**Signal Hopping**

The angry supernova of Betelgeuse
live-streaming has begun in this place
where even small victories
can be hard won.

Send me telepathic messages from
a place far brighter than the sun—
conflicting feelings explode inside but
you can't Bluetooth or WiFi your way
out of this one,
Hedy Lamar!



**Ron Myers** wrote his first poems at Indiana University in the 1970s. In San Francisco, Ron workshopped his poems with Harold Norse, Neeli Cherkovski and Clive Matson. His subjects include environmental causes, ancient world cultures, geography (exterior/interior), and love and its frustrations. Ron was recently appointed the National Beat Poetry Foundation's Poet Laureate for California for 2024 -2026. His poems have appeared in The Slant, The Scribbler, Beatdom, The Brooklyn Rail and over a dozen anthologies in the U.S., England, France and Italy.

## Catherine Katey Johnson

## A Woman's Love

All those hugs and memories of hugs
sage, cedar and pinion-burning
exploring the high desert with your grandkids.
Your mother living long enough to appreciate you,
and you, to appreciate her.
Standing atop a volcano at daybreak
with a rainbow around your shadow on a cloud.
Disco, line, and slow dancing
Singing and laughing
at the concert with your bestie--
the two of you stage-front holding each of The Boss' legs.
The lessons, the talents shared and indulged.
It's hot, molten love with a star-crossed Pisces,
the super bowl ring, the adventure
the early-bird special with your friends from high school.
It's the warmth of your dog, snuggled up with you in bed on
a chilly night.
Seeing your kids become caring adults
and being the recipient of their care.
The friend who is at the other end of the phone when you
have a meltdown.
The one who helps you sift through the weather-beaten-memories
tossed out in the yard when the roof caved in.
It's purposeful rage
and boundaries.
Casting your ballot.
A garden, ready to harvest,
bees and bats and ice caps intact,
sharing and caring,
and a hand helping you up,
telling you to take your rightful place on the throne.

**Catherine Katey Johnson** Award-winning Author and screenwriter; a Woody Guthrie poet and New Generation Beat poet living in Cushing, OK. Her poems are in many anthologies and three of her own collections. Her latest screenplay is a parody of Clint Eastwood's body of work, titled, MAGNUM FARCE.

## A.M. Hayden

### Hugging Nun at the Sacre Coeur

you can tell by the way they dress
and by the history clinging to their soaked lips and lashes
floors slick with stomps of rain boots and pointed
umbrellas snapping shut, spraying droplets onto dark coats
faces with closed eyes and open mouths
unrequested baptisms as they kneel in every direction
candle-lit prayers caressing saint statues' frozen feet
genuflecting since womb's holy waters, since Joan of Arc
charged with her 4th century sword,
since pagan ancestors invoked
under crone's tree canopies, since this smiling, plump nun
in front of you beams like morning light lifts the horizon
you can tell by the way she dressed
in habit and by the herstory cradled between her vowed lips
and rosehip cheeks,
and you have a sudden overwhelming urge
to reach out your sodden hands to her powder soft, robed
French arms
for her to hold you like she is Amma,
the Indian hugging saint
but you remember the French aren't really known
for hugging
no thunderstorms either
mostly just misting like London,
Seattle, just hug-less damp dreaming

**A.M. Hayden** is the Poet Laureate and Professor for Sinclair College in Ohio. Her debut collection, American Saunter, released December 2024 (FlowerSong Press). Her first chapbook, How to Tie Tobacco, and second collection, Old World Wings, releases 2025 (Wild Ink Publishing). Hayden is a Pushcart Prize nominee and the 2023 River Heron Editor's Choice Prize winner.  She lives with her family and many furry rescue babies, including a very special blind, three-legged pup named Vinny Valentine.

## RescuePoetix | Susan Justiniano

## Title Machinations of Sacred Silence

There is something sacred in silence
a harmonic understanding of the world
power to define our civilized selves
connections between us and …

THEM
The heart –
the first THEM
Currents feeding the rest

Flow in
Flow out
Thump
Thump

Rushing through silence
confident, sure with its mission:
Need to reach

THEM

The brain –
structured THEM

externalizing power to systems
that don't always give back
false witness to how we think the world is

rationalizing for

THEM

The soul –
the biggest THEM

succession of self
unpredictable in rebellion of THEM
always looking inward
to change the outward

sacred silence is busy



**RescuePoetix - Susan Justiniano** is a self-taught bilingual, internationally published performing poet, workshop facilitator, teaching and recording artist based in New Jersey. She is twice honored Poet Laureate: first Puerto Rican Poet Laureate (Jersey City, NJ 2020-2022), State of NJ Beat Poet Laureate (2022-2024). She develops a body of work focused on community and social justice.
https://linktr.ee/rescuepoetix

**Virginia Shreve**

**The Song is Fire; The Steps are Wind; Poem of the Girl Not
Believed, but Not Defeated**

My hair is red
assaults perfect space
like flames licking cathedrals

like my space, perfect
was assaulted

I wear my insides outside
like a tattered cape
of dead birds, the plumage faded
once the light escaped
my heart is laid open

Yet still
each fierce night
Again I swallow the moon, the stars, the held breath of night
light shoots from my fingertips
and against the dark

I dance


**Virginia Shreve**, Beat Poet Laureate of CT 2020 - 2022 and current Town of Canton, CT Poet Laureate, resides in the small river town of Collinsville, CT with husband and dogs, none well-trained, but all good-natured. Her poems have appeared in The Southern Poetry Review, Slippery Elm, Naugatuck River Review, Phantom Drift, Your Daily Poem (online) and others, including numerous anthologies.

**Jayati Roy**

**A Divine Encounter,**
(based on a true event)

She wears a nose ring.
Red and round – like a hoop of fire,
Her eyes scintillate,
A thousand diamonds
Piercing the evening sky.

Doe-eyed and captivating,
Hypnotic and devious,
Her skin, polished and glistening
Neither pitch black nor white,
But pearly silver-
As if kissed by the moon on a dark night.
I see her next to me.

I am paralyzed. My limbs weaken.
A constellation of thoughts cajole –
"Who are you?"
I blurt out.
"You cannot be real."

"You don't know me," she whispers,
Her thin lips contorted,
stretched like a rubber band pulled tight, ready to snap.

Jolted from sleep,
I mumble something foolish.
She erupts into laughter –
Loud, hearty, thunderous.

The earth trembles.
I feel dizzy,
Adrift.

Her thin red lips curl into a smile.
"Fourteen generations of your family have paid me homage,
Yet you are lost."
Her eyes shimmer,
Like diamonds in dark room,
She smiles, a deadly sort of smile.

"Kali Ma?"
"Kali Ma?"

"Is it you? You?"
A cold sweat trickles down my brow,
My knees quiver.

…and then she laughs,
Moving from side to side,
Her long black tresses that fall down to her waist
Swing in the air like blades of a fan.
My legs stiffen and my jaws tighten.

"Will you come to see me?"
I stare in silence.
"In heaven?" I manage to murmur, a while later.
"Oh no.
It's too early."

A 'to-do' list flits through my mind.
Please wait.
What's the hurry?
The words choke in my throat.
I feel a chill even in my marrow.

Yet, I nod perfunctorily,
Delirious,
Betrayed by my own fears.

Is this a dream?
She has no right to invite me like this.
Is she Kali Ma really?

Goddess of Time and Death,
Consort of Lord Siva -
"Oh Goddess, why me," I plead.

Yet, even in my drowsy, hazy, state,
I bow: a ritual woven into my DNA,
Imbued by the spirit of my ancestors.

"I shall send you a ticket."
She grins and then vanishes.
Oh God! Is my end near, I wonder?

…A year later…
At a conference in Bangkok someone mentions cheap tickets to Calcutta,
India.
It's a sign, I implore,
Let me see, what's in store?

Her fragrance permeates the air,
Traps my soul.
The yellow garlands drape every inch of her sacred body –
Yet, her eyes glisten and smile.
In a little temple in Kalighat,
in the outskirts of Calcutta I stand,
drenched in the impermanence of life
and the fragility of the spirit,
I bow before her: who is not just woman or shakti,
But both warrior and saviour.
The waves of the Ganges murmur in my ears,
A gentle, cool breeze grazes my face.
I listen to the priests who chant in rhythmic fervour,
Sandalwood incense thick in the air- its scent cling to my breath.

I am not dreaming.
Kali Ma, you kept your word.
A tune hums in my mind.
Her laughter blooms like a rose,

As I kneel in prayer.
I close my eyes – her presence enfolds me.

"It has been a long time."
A voice echoes in the distance.
I am home.


**Jayati Roy** is a retired professor who has had a colourful career in both academia and the corporate sector. She has travelled widely, the latest being to Antarctica and South America. Her passion is in writing short stories and poetry that delve on stories of the past.

## Barbara Shepherd

### Wonder Woman

In the early years while hubby traveled for work,
my young shoulders carried the load of mom and dad.
That continued when his work changed to local, and
more problems surfaced.
Parental and domestic issues - unresolvable.
Divorce slivered in.

As a single mom, I worked to jobs from daylight
until almost dawn to pay bills.
When my teenagers demanded extras, I had to respond
I'm doing the best I can. I'm not Wonder Woman today.

Over the years, I battled pain, fear, and financial strife.
I faced the surgeon's knife for a hysterectomy,
back, hip, and shoulder surgeries,
three kinds of cancer, and more.
I survived serious infections, pneumonia,
and RSV, and have enough metal parts and
broken bones to qualify as an athlete.

In spite of all that, I own my home and
retired from a late career in public service.
Discovering creativity, I became an
award-winning artist, and a published author
with hundreds of writing awards.

My Lord brought me through all those tough
times and the positive ones.
He let me witness my boys become successful
and kind young men with families of their own.
I'm reminded my grandchildren need me, too.

The paperweight my son gave me after he became
an adult caught my eye.
Its message - "Wonder Woman Works Here."

Recovering from an illness now, I choose to be
Wonder Woman again, the woman I always was.



**Barbara Shepherd**, an award-winning poet/writer/artist from Oklahoma is a Woody Guthrie Poet, Poetry Society of Oklahoma's Poet Laureate, State of Oklahoma Poet Laureate Nominee, and Oklahoma State Fair's Voice of the Fair Poet. She wrote Night of Terror, Vittles and Vignettes, Patchwork Skin, River Bend, The Potbelly Pig Promise, Secrets from None Such Road, and co-wrote Reach for the Clouds. Her poems and prose are published in anthologies, poetry journals, and online. www.barbarashepherd.com

## CR Montoya

## Remembering RBG

"Mom taught me to always be a lady…"
independent, confident, and willing to run throughbarriers.

I grew along the way, striving to
work for what I believed in.
Grow throughout your journey,
stand firm for your values.

Learn to pick your battles,
not for winning - to let justice thrive.

Never burn your bridges,
old bridges help us to win the day.

Think about what you want,
then do the work to attain it.
Enjoy what you do
with your whole heart and mind.

"As you grow, bring along your crew,"
those you trust and rely on.
You will flourish together.

"Don't say women's rights
stand on the constitutional principle
of equal citizenship stature for men and women."

What you view as an impediment
can be something great
that brings you good fortune.
It's up to you.

With a steadfast heart
women attain power
and barriers crumble.

Fight for what you care about
leading others to join
on your quest.

Everest is just another mountain.
Climb it without fear
someone will be there to guide you.

"Women belong in all places where decisions are being made.
It shouldn't be that women are the exception."
Women's insights should be the norm.

"Never underestimate a girl
    with a book."

The quotes are those of Justice Ruth Bader Ginsberg.
The sentiments reflect her genius and will.


**CR Montoya**
Papa The Happy Snowman narrates a series of children's stories by CR Montoya. CR has published children's tales featuring Papa and other characters since 2012. He is actively involved in the Long Island poetry scene and has contributed to anthologies such as Nassau County Voices in Verse, several BardsAnthologies, and others. One of his favorite stories is Sophie's Unicorn: A Tale of Wonder. CR enjoys the outdoors and often explores the wooded areas near his home in Long Island, NY. Astronomy is another passion that has inspired some of his work.

## Mary Eichhorn Fletcher

## Edith

"I made gardens and parks and planted all kinds of fruit trees in them." Ecclesiastes 2:5

It was poetry I was born with.
(Poetry was in my heart
from my beginning.)

My mother was unhappy with her creation and
that her creation created
her own and different creation.

She made me put away my poems.
I began to write in darkness.

After a while
I preferred the light
and she sent me to New York and Paris
to learn to scribble other things.
But in my heart it was always poetry.

I started anew but not with
pen and paper.
I crafted carefully.
Away from my cities of light
I traveled into
the sunlight of my home.
I plotted out
where every patch of flowers
would nestle against stone walkways.
I angulated the position
of each yew so it would align and
guide a weary soul
along paths to peace.

I painted poems tree by tree,
and rhymed terraces with
clouds.

Through the window in my bedroom
I looked down and watched
my book of poems grow.
Each row of Spanish bluebells became
a metered sonnet
with pink and purple phlox
the couplet at its close.
I drank in the May garden's perfumes
when lilacs and viburnum
mingled their fragrances and sang,
in loving psalms, praises to their creator.

Sometimes now, at night,
when birdsong disappears
into the darkness and
when busyness of bees
goes away and
sweet smells of early roses
climb through my open window –
I lie in bed and wonder
what poetry I might have written if
my mother had laughed
in love at my childish verses –
and bought a leather journal
with vellum paper for my work.
What might she think of my sestinas
and versi sciotti (row upon row)
made from daisies and lilies and
long lavender spikes?

Author's note: Edith Newbold Jones Wharton was born in 1862 and died in 1937. She was an American poet and novelist but is better known for her novels. Her mother never encouraged her to write poetry. She was 16 when her father had her poems published.

**Mary Eichhorn Fletcher** lives in a small town in Connecticut with her husband (and the occasional cat who wanders through and decides to stay). She has been writing poetry since she entered first grade. In 1997 she began to study the Bible. Her poetry and other work are frequently informed by her faith and by her love of nature. Fletcher is also an avid letter writer and may be reached by email at AtticMary@gmail.com

**Chrysavgi Kapella-Papadimitrio**

**Through Woman Springs the Greatest!**
(Ancient Greek Maxim)

Eve, God called her by His voice,
and her purpose was a sacred choice.
She gives life, the earth sustains,
the source where greatness still remains.

Her virtues shine like beams of light,
spreading wide and burning bright.
An angel, strong and ever near,
a guiding hand, a voice sincere,
a timeless sign of love profound,
of strength and hope that knows no bound!

---

They said: A woman's heart so deep,
a boundless chasm, secrets keep...
Yet SHE, the Virgin, pure and bright,
prays for us to find the light!

Harsh were laws that held her tight,
shackled dreams and stole her right.
But time has turned, the world has changed,
her rightful place is now reclaimed.

Through struggles fought, the battle won,
from hidden halls, she saw the sun,
and on time's path she carved her way,
her place in life is here to stay.

---

She fought, she conquered, scaled the skies,
and reached the stars where glory lies.
She charmed, inspired, with fearless might,

and claimed her throne in history's light.

Rebel, ruler, mother, friend,
a force that legends now commend.
Cleopatra, Aspasia's grace,
Olympias, Joan's embrace.

Some called her a devil, others divine,
a narcissus, a rose, a cactus with spine.
Yet always, through all that they could see,
a flower she would always be!
---

Oh, woman!
Never forget, or you shall fall…
Your virtues shine, outshine them all!
Man may stand both strong and free,
but you, dear woman, hold the key!

**Chrysavgi Kapella-Papadimitriou** was born in Sykourio, Larissa, and currently resides in Larissa. She is an award-winning poet and writer, recognized in international and national literary competitions. She has received poetry awards from the International Art Academy, the Fountoulis Conservatory in Volos, and the K.P. Kavafia competition, as well as short story awards from the literary magazine "Deucalion the Thessalian."Since 2008, she has been publishing in literary journals and actively participating in poetry events.

**Paul Richmond**

**Goddess Hecate - heh·kuh·tee**

A Greek Goddess
The Goddess of magic
Our guide through darkness
Exists in all realms at once
Seeing in all directions

Responsibly respecting boundaries
A protector against evil
Appearing at crossroads

Where are you when we need you
Have you become
Disgusted with what you see
Have you concluded
There is no magic strong enough
To save us from
Stupidity
Our lust for power and greed
Self-destruction

Are there any malevolent curses
To stop the madness
Or does that only continue the violence

You have been called a witch
Seen as antisocial
Rebellious
Independent
Refusing to be dominated
By male oppression
Have you become overwhelmed
Are you hiding with the covers over your head
Hoping as many of us are
That when we wake up
The bad dream will have passed

For those who have woken up
This bad dream has been our history
That some want to deny and continues

In our daily rituals
Summon Hecate within us
Gather the tribe together
For we can't do it alone
It's time to create magic

**Paul Richmond** was awarded Beat Poet Laureate by National Beat Poetry Foundation for, MA 2017-2019, USA 2019-2020, & Lifetime 2022. He performs nationally and internationally, solo and with "Do It Now." He has eight books, more info www.humanerrorpublishing.com

## Lesley Constable

### Brave Women

Brave women, for many necessary reasons,
plunge defenseless fingers into
the mouths of very young children with sharp, pointy teeth. Often, they
suckle the same. This sometimes does not work out well. They know this
going in.

Brave women mop up all blood types from all wounds and orifices no matter
how repugnant, answer impossible questions with "yes," and "I understand"
when they don't, comfort the raw nerves of a friend when their own are raw
and, if and when called upon, push out the sometimes very large heads of
their offspring and yell and scream because this fucking hurts.

Brave women yell and scream anyhow in many situations and for many
reasons. It is when they reach that shrill high point. And, only they know
when that moment is hot upon them. It is private.
Brave women are sometimes mistaken for something else, especially when
they scream for reasons unclear. But, do not forget, it is the screamers
who are the bravest of brave women…to give voice, to give shape, to give meaning through sound to that which

they don't understand - or- understand way too much.
A brave woman never has to tell anything to anybody that she doesn't want
to. It is a secret. Her secret that has sound or no sound, at all,….if she
chooses.
Is it love? Is the heart of a brave woman only about love?

Some would say
yes.

And, some would absolutely avoid any further knowledge, reference or
inquiry regarding any particular high point, of any woman, especially if she
is "a screamer."

Brave women sob at weddings and funerals giving a different voice to that
which is simply too much. Too much.
And it is that sound, only - of a brave woman sobbing -
that quiets us all,
quiets us all better than lullabies.

Because that sound is life, simply that.
Brave women love you and aren't you the lucky one to be loved by a brave
woman?
They are your mothers, your sisters, your aunts, grandmothers, cousins,
neighbors, friends, your lovers. Watchful, paying attention, laughing for us,
at us, with us.

The laughter of brave women is the music we dance to,
the music of our souls
in our bodies
to which we spin.


**Lesley Constable** - Poet/painter Lesley Constable crosses borders. A US/UK citizen by birth, she lives in Santa Fe, NM (USA), Margate, UK and Sayulita, Mexico, is a life-long rock 'n' roll hippie chick, road-tripper, trained modern dancer, was an arts journalist/art critic, University studio arts assoc. professor, art gallery curator, published in US/UK anthologies (since 1999). "Entry Point" (2015) is available online. "Border Songs, a House without Walls," is soon to be published.

## Amb Dr Priyanka Neogi

### Role of Women

Women, you just keep your role, if you understand a little more, it's the best.
You cover the world with compassion,
Riddles, fetters, and tortures pervade you in your arranged world,
Look, you have the solution.
You have become precious in the change of era,
You have taken away your rights by fighting against time.
You have explained that you are also good at war.
May you go ahead and give a shout of victory.
Just keep the skills -
"In education, profession, technology, sports, culture and politics"
Just stay strong and tremble.
Don't go short in anything, so what's the fear!
Leave fair, keep strong.
This night is yours, this society is yours, your freedom is your hand.
Why else paws in your kingdom!
Why give the extended and developed night in the hands of others!
You mother you can "teach to respect and honor to women",
You can "change the world of women" through your education,
"To stir the world of women".


**Amb Dr.Priyanka Neogi** is from West Bengal state,India. She is a professional business woman, librarian, teacher, international poet, writer, short film writer, researcher, columnist, editor, plus many more. She is versatile and multi talented, and a National & International Awardee.

## David Henri

## Venus

In the dark of night,
imperceivable sunlight passes around the planet into space,
reflecting lunar luminosity radiantly
         from the earth shaded orb of crescent moon onto
my love's face,
who then reflects the moonlight rendered of reflected sun rays
                                                                into
my perception,
all the stars send twinkles adorning her hair with sparkling sequences,
say, look right up there,
it is Venus dazzling stunning in bedazzled sky,
there she is alright, basking totally exposed in the sun lit night,
her tiny silhouette is a magically mirrored image transported by light
                                                                into
my love's eyes,
carrying a spell of seduction
the beautiful yellow tinted spherical goddess of love and beauty
  is being mysteriously shone into my sweetheart's pupils
                          prompting an unveiling of a
universal truth,
in fact,
my very own wife shares the xx chromosomes
         of the actual model who posed for Venus DeMilo,
as all women on mother earth share this biological phenomenon,
each a holy beautiful goddess in starlit splendor
                                  exhibiting alluring attributes of femininity,
with moonshine on cheeks and Venus glowing in wonderous eyes

**David Henri** lives in New Hartford CT. He writes about communing with nature, sustainable living and connecting to the cosmos. The podcaster Rich Cyr once introduced him as Emerson meets
Timothy Leary. He has published four short poetry collections.

## Roxanne Hoffman

### Saltitos del Corazón, Otra Vez /
### Little Skips of the Heart, Again

two
friends,
women,
slow tango
in step with their hearts,
rejoice in lives shared, children raised.
divorced, widowed, they glide store aisles,
feather empty nests
as pregnant
daughter
comes
home



**Roxanne Hoffman** New Jersey-based poet, runs the independent literary press Poets Wear Prada with Jack Cooper. Her words can be found in cyberspace (The Performance

Poetry Preservation Project, Scarlet Literary Magazine, and HIV: Here & Now); set to music (David Morneau's Love Songs); on the silver screen (2005 indie flick Love and the Vampire); and in print (The Bandana Republic: A Literary Anthology by Gang Members and Their Affiliates and, most recently, Whisper Whisper Shout: A When Women Speak Anthology).

## The National Beat Poetry Foundation, Inc.

I founded the National Beat Poetry Foundation, Inc. to bring different perspectives to how people view the beat poets. I feel a great injustice was done in the past. My goal is tobring people together through poetry, art and music. Changethe negative views and warped truths of beat poets into apositive image. I try to focus on the natural world, respect all forms of life, and help preserve what is left of the wild spaces and the Earth itself. We are all interconnected to each other. Our words matter. The beat laureates in my organization are trying to be better versions of themselves by doing gooin this world. I'm building a new generation of beat poets. Freedom and growth and giving all people a voice. I did notexperience that in traditional poetry circles. I wasn't accepted there.

To me the word Beat means to keep evolving.

Debbie Tosun Kilday
Owner/CEO
National Beat Poetry Foundation, Inc. & its Festivals

If you would like to help, go to:
http://paypal.me/NationalBeatPoetry

Website:
http://nationalbeatpoetryfoundation.org

Find us on Facebook,
YouTube: https://www.youtube.com/@nationalbeatpoetryfoundati5845/videos
X(@BeatPoetryFest)

Instagram (dtkbeatpoetnbpf)

Look for our publications: New Generation Beat Publications Online Magazine - BeatLife.org

Email: nbpf15@gmail.coe

www.ingramcontent.com/pod-product-compliance
Lightning Source LLC
Chambersburg PA
CBHW062226080426
42734CB00010B/2041